Irenaeus Against Heresies, V3

Irenaeus

Table of Contents

Table of Contents

Irenaeus Against Heresies, V3

Table of Contents

Irenaeus Against Heresies, V3

Irenaeus Against Heresies, V3

Irenaeus

- BOOK III.

  - PREFACE.
  - CHAP. I.—THE APOSTLES DID NOT COMMENCE TO PREACH THE GOSPEL, OR TO PLACE ANYTHING ON RECORD, UNTIL THEY WERE ENDOWED WITH THE GIFTS AND POWER OF THE HOLY SPIRIT. THEY PREACHED ONE GOD ALONE, MAKER OF HEAVEN AND EARTH.
  - CHAP. II.—THE HERETICS FOLLOW NEITHER SCRIPTURE NOR TRADITION.
  - CHAP. III.—A REFUTATION OF THE HERETICS, FROM THE FACT THAT, IN THE VARIOUS CHURCHES, A PERPETUAL SUCCESSION OF BISHOPS WAS KEPT UP.
  - CHAP. IV.—THE TRUTH IS TO BE FOUND NOWHERE ELSE BUT IN THE CATHOLIC CHURCH, THE SOLE DEPOSITORY OF APOSTOLICAL DOCTRINE. HERESIES ARE OF RECENT FORMATION, AND CANNOT TRACE THEIR ORIGIN UP TO THE APOSTLES.
  - CHAP. V. — CHRIST AND HIS APOSTLES, WITHOUT ANY FRAUD, DECEPTION, OR HYPOCRISY, PREACHED THAT ONE GOD, THE FATHER, WAS THE FOUNDER OF ALL THINGS. THEY DID NOT ACCOMMODATE THEIR DOCTRINETO THE PREPOSSESSIONS OF THEIR HEARERS.
  - CHAP. VI — THE HOLY GHOST, THROUGHOUT THE OLD TESTAMENT SCRIPTURES, MADE MENTION OF NO OTHER GOD OR LORD, SAVE HIM WHO IS THE TRUE GOD.
  - CHAP. VII. — REPLY TO AN OBJECTION FOUNDED ON THE WORDS OF ST. PAUL (2 Cor. IV. 5). ST. PAUL OCCASIONALLY USES WORDS NOT IN THEIR GRAMMATICAL, SEQUENCE.

AS DISTINCT BEINGS; NEITHER CAN IT BE ALLEGED THAT THE SON OF GOD BECAME MAN MERELY IN APPEARANCE, BUT THAT HE DID SO TRULY AND ACTUALLY.

BOOK III.

PREFACE.

THOU hast indeed enjoined upon me, my very dear friend, that I should bring to light the Valentinian doctrines, concealed, as their votaries imagine; that I should exhibit their diversity, and compose a treatise in refutation of them. therefore have undertaken—showing that they spring from Simon, the father of all heretics—to exhibit both their doctrines and successions, and to set forth arguments against them all. Wherefore, since the conviction of these men and their exposure is in many points but one work, I have sent unto thee [certain] books, of which the first comprises the opinions of all these men, and exhibits their customs, and the character of their behaviour. In the second, again, their perverse teachings are cast down and overthrown, and, such as they really are, laid bare and open to view. But in this, the third book I shall adduce proofs from the Scriptures, so that I may come behind in nothing of what thou hast enjoined; yea, that over and above what thou didst reckon upon, thou mayest receive from me the means of combating and vanquishing those who, in whatever manner, are propagating falsehood. For the love of God, being rich and ungrudging, confers upon the suppliant more than he can ask from it. Call to mind then, the things which I have stated in the two preceding books, and, taking these in connection with them, thou shalt have from me a very copious refutation of all the heretics; and faithfully and strenuously shalt thou resist them in defence of the only true and life–giving faith, which the Church has received from the apostles and imparted to her sons. For the Lord of all gave to His apostles the power of the Gospel, through whom also we have known the truth, that is, the doctrine of the Son of God; to whom also did the Lord declare: "He that heareth you, heareth Me; and he that despiseth you, despiseth Me, and Him that sent Me."(1)

CHAP. I.—THE APOSTLES DID NOT COMMENCE TO PREACH THE GOSPEL, OR TO PLACE ANYTHING ON RECORD, UNTIL THEY WERE ENDOWED WITH THE GIFTS AND POWER OF THE HOLY SPIRIT. THEY PREACHED ONE GOD ALONE, MAKER OF HEAVEN AND EARTH.

1. WE have learned from none others the plan of our salvation, than from those through whom the Gospel has come down to us, which they did at one time proclaim in public, and, at a later period, by the will of God, handed down to us in the Scriptures, to be the ground and pillar of our faith.(2) For it is unlawful to assert that they preached before they possessed "perfect knowledge," as some do even venture to say, boasting themselves as improvers of the apostles. For, after our Lord rose from the dead, [the apostles] were invested with power from on high when the Holy Spirit came down [upon them], were filled from all [His gifts], and had perfect knowledge: they departed to the ends of the earth, preaching the glad tidings of the good things [sent] from God to us, and proclaiming the peace of heaven to men, who indeed do all equally and individually possess the Gospel of God. Matthew also issued a written Gospel among the Hebrews(3) in their own dialect, while Peter and Paul were preaching at Rome, and laying the foundations of the Church. After their departure, Mark, the disciple and interpreter of Peter, did also hand down to us in writing what had been preached by Peter. Luke also, the companion of Paul, recorded in a book the Gospel preached by him. Afterwards, John, the disciple of the Lord, who also had leaned upon His breast, did himself publish a Gospel during his residence at Ephesus in Asia.

2. These have all declared to us that there is one God, Creator of heaven and earth, announced by the law and the prophets; and one Christ the Son of God. If any one do not agree to these truths, he despises the companions of the Lord; nay more, he despises Christ Himself the Lord; yea, he despises the Father also, and stands self–condemned, resisting and opposing his own salvation, as is the case with all heretics.

CHAP. II.—THE HERETICS FOLLOW NEITHER SCRIPTURE NOR TRADITION.

1. When, however, they are confuted from the Scriptures, they turn round and accuse these same Scriptures, as if they were not correct, nor of authority, and [assert] that they are ambiguous, and that the truth cannot be extracted from them by those who are ignorant of tradition. For [they allege] that the truth was not delivered by means of written documents, but viva voce: wherefore also Paul declared, "But we speak wisdom among those that are perfect, but not the wisdom of this world."(1) And this wisdom each one of them alleges to be the fiction of his own inventing, forsooth; so that, according to their idea, the truth properly resides at one time in Valentinus, at another in Marcion, at

another in Cerinthus, then afterwards in Basilides, or has even been indifferently in any other opponent,(2) who could speak nothing pertaining to salvation. For every one of these men, being altogether of a perverse disposition, depraving the system of truth, is not ashamed to preach himself.

2. But, again, when we refer them to that tradition which originates from the apostles, [and] which is preserved by means of the succession of presbyters in the Churches, they object to tradition, saying that they themselves are wiser not merely than the presbyters, but even than the apostles, because they have discovered the unadulterated truth. For [they maintain] that the apostles intermingled the things of the law with the words of the Saviour; and that not the apostles alone, but even the Lord Himself, spoke as at one time from the Demiurge, at another from the intermediate place, and yet again from the Pleroma, but that they themselves, indubitably, unsulliedly, and purely, have knowledge of the hidden mystery: this is, indeed, to blaspheme their Creator after a most impudent manner! It comes to this, therefore, that these men do now consent neither to Scripture nor to tradition.

3. Such are the adversaries with whom we have to deal, my very dear friend, endeavouring like slippery serpents to escape at all points. Where– fore they must be opposed at all points, if per– chance, by cutting off their retreat, we may succeed in turning them back to the truth. For, though it is not an easy thing for a soul under the influence of error to repent, yet, on the other hand, it is not altogether impossible to escape from error when the truth is brought alongside it.

CHAP. III.—A REFUTATION OF THE HERETICS, FROM THE FACT THAT, IN THE VARIOUS CHURCHES, A PERPETUAL SUCCESSION OF BISHOPS WAS KEPT UP.

1. It is within the power of all, therefore, in every Church, who may wish to see the truth, to contemplate clearly the tradition of the apostles manifested throughout the whole world; and we are in a position to reckon up those who were by the apostles instituted bishops in the Churches, and [to demonstrate] the succession of these men to our own times; those who neither taught nor knew of anything like what these [heretics] rave about. For if the apostles had known hidden mysteries, which they were in the habit of imparting to "the perfect" apart and privily from the rest, they would have delivered them

6

especially to those to whom they were also committing the Churches themselves. For they were desirous that these men should be very perfect and blameless in all things, whom also they were leaving behind as their successors, delivering up their own place of government to these men; which men, if they discharged their functions honestly, would be a great boon [to the Church], but if they should fall away, the direst calamity.

2. Since, however, it would be very tedious, in such a volume as this, to reckon up the successions of all the Churches, we do put to confusion all those who, in whatever manner, whether by an evil self–pleasing, by vainglory, or by blindness and perverse opinion, assemble in unauthorized meetings; [we do this, I say,] by indicating that tradition derived from the apostles, of the very great, the very ancient, and universally known Church founded and organized at Rome by the two most glorious apostles, Peter and Paul; as also [by pointing out] the faith preached to men, which comes down to our time by means of the successions of the bishops. For it is a matter of necessity that every Church should agree with this Church, on account of its pre– eminent authority,(3) that is, the faithful every– where, inasmuch as the apostolical tradition has been preserved continuously by those [faithful men] who exist everywhere.

3. The blessed apostles, then, having founded and built up the Church, committed into the hands of Linus the office of the episcopate. Of this Linus, Paul makes mention in the Epistles to Timothy. To him succeeded Anacletus; and after him, in the third place from the apostles, Clement was allotted the bishopric. This man, as he had seen the blessed apostles, and had been conversant with them, might be said to have the preaching of the apostles still echoing [in his ears], and their traditions before his eyes. Nor was he alone [in this], for there were many still remaining who had received instructions from the apostles. In the time of this Clement, no small dissension having occurred among the brethren at Corinth, the Church in Rome despatched a most powerful letter to the Corinthians, exhorting them to peace, renewing their faith, and declaring the tradition which it had lately received from the apostles, proclaiming the one God, omnipotent, the Maker of heaven and earth, the Creator of man, who brought on the deluge, and called Abraham, who led the people from the land of Egypt, spake with Moses, set forth the law, sent the prophets, and who has prepared fire for the devil and his angels. From this document, whosoever chooses to do so, may learn that He, the Father of our Lord Jesus Christ, was preached by the Churches, and may also understand the apostolical tradition of the Church, since this Epistle is of older date than these men who are now propagating falsehood, and who conjure into existence another god beyond the Creator and the Maker

of all existing things. To this Clement there succeeded Evaristus. Alexander followed Evaristus; then, sixth from the apostles, Sixtus was appointed; after him, Telephorus, who was gloriously martyred; then Hyginus; after him, Pius; then after him, Anicetus. Sorer having succeeded Anicetus, Eleutherius does now, in the twelfth place from the apostles, hold the inheritance of the episcopate. In this order, and by this succession, the ecclesiastical tradition from the apostles, and the preaching of the truth, have come down to us. And this is most abundant proof that there is one and the same vivifying faith, which has been preserved in the Church from the apostles until now, and handed down in truth.

4. But Polycarp also was not only instructed by apostles, and conversed with many who had seen Christ, but was also, by apostles in Asia, appointed bishop of the Church in Smyrna, whom I also saw in my early youth, for he tarried [on earth] a very long time, and, when a very old man, gloriously and most nobly suffering

martyrdom,(1) departed this life, having always taught the things which he had learned from the apostles, and which the Church has handed down, and which alone are true. To these things all the Asiatic Churches testify, as do also those men who have succeeded Polycarp down to the present time,—a man who was of much greater weight, and a more stedfast witness of truth, than Valentinus, and Marcion, and the rest of the heretics. He it was who, coming to Rome in the time of Anicetus caused many to turn away from the aforesaid heretics to the Church of God, proclaiming that he had received this one and sole truth from the apostles,—that, namely, which is handed down by the Church.(2) There are also those who heard from him that John, the disciple of the Lord, going to bathe at Ephesus, and perceiving Cerinthus within, rushed out of the bath–house without bathing, exclaiming, "Let us fly, lest even the bath–house fall down, because Cerinthus, the enemy of the truth, is within." And Polycarp himself replied to Marcion, who met him on one occasion, and said, "Dost thou know me?" "I do know thee, the first–born of Satan." Such was the horror which the apostles and their disciples had against holding even verbal communication with any corrupters of the truth; as Paul also says, "A man that is an heretic, after the first and second admonition, reject; knowing that he that is such is subverted, and sinneth, being condemned of himself."(3) There is also a very powerful(4) Epistle of Polycarp written to the Philippians, from which those who choose to do so, and are anxious about their salvation, can learn the character of his faith, and the preaching of the truth. Then, again, the Church in Ephesus, founded by Paul, and having John remaining among them permanently until the times of Trajan, is a true witness of the tradition of the apostles.

CHAP. IV.—THE TRUTH IS TO BE FOUND NOWHERE ELSE BUT IN THE CATHOLIC CHURCH, THE SOLE DEPOSITORY OF APOSTOLICAL DOCTRINE. HERESIES ARE OF RECENT FORMATION, AND CANNOT TRACE THEIR ORIGIN UP TO THE APOSTLES.

1. Since therefore we have such proofs, it is not necessary to seek the truth among others which it is easy to obtain from the Church; since the apostles, like a rich man [depositing his money] in a bank, lodged in her hands most copiously all things pertaining to the truth: so that every man, whosoever will, can draw from her the water of life.(1) For she is the entrance to life; all others are thieves and robbers. On this account are we bound to avoid them, but to make choice of the thing pertaining to the Church with the utmost diligence, and to lay hold of the tradition of the truth. For how stands the case? Suppose there arise a dispute relative to some important question(2) among us, should we not have recourse to the most ancient Churches with which the apostles held constant intercourse, and learn from them what is certain and clear in regard to the present question? For how should it be if the apostles themselves had not left us writings? Would it not be necessary, [in that case,] to follow the course of the tradition which they handed down to those to whom they did commit the Churches?

2. To which course many nations of those barbarians who believe in Christ do assent, having salvation written in their hearts by the Spirit, without paper or ink, and, carefully preserving the ancient tradition,(3) believing in one God, the Creator of heaven and earth, and all things therein, by means of Christ Jesus, the Son of God; who, because of His surpassing love towards His creation, condescended to be born of the virgin, He Himself uniting man through Himself to God, and having suffered under Pontius Pilate, and rising again, and having been received up in splendour, shall come in glory, the Saviour of those who are saved, and the Judge of those who are judged, and sending into eternal fire those who transform the truth, and despise His Father and His advent. Those who, in the absence of written documents,(4) have believed this faith, are barbarians, so far as regards our language; but as regards doctrine, manner, and tenor of life, they are, because of faith, very wise indeed; and they do please God, ordering their conversation in all

9

righteousness, chastity, and wisdom. If any one were to preach to these men the inventions of the heretics, speaking to them in their own language, they would at once stop their ears, and flee as far off as possible, not enduring even to listen to the blasphemous address. Thus, by means of that ancient tradition of the apostles, they do not suffer their mind to conceive anything of the [doctrines suggested by the] portentous language of these teachers, among whom neither Church nor doctrine has ever been established.

3. For, prior to Valentinus, those who follow Valentinus had no existence; nor did those from Marcion exist before Marcion; nor, in short, had

any of those malignant—minded people, whom I have above enumerated, any being previous to the initiators and inventors of their perversity. For Valentinus came to Rome in the time of Hyginus, flourished under Pius, and remained until Anicetus. Cerdon, too, Marcion's predecessor, himself arrived in the time of Hyginus, who was the ninth bishop.(5) Coming frequently into the Church, and making public confession, he thus remained, one time teaching in secret, and then again making public confession; but at last, having been denounced for corrupt teaching, he was excommunicated(6) from the assembly of the brethren. Marcion, then, succeeding him, flourished under Anicetus, who held the tenth place of the episcopate. But the rest, who are called Gnostics, take rise from Menander, Simon's disciple, as I have shown; and each one of them appeared to be both the father and the high priest of that doctrine into which he has been initiated. But all these (the Marcosians) broke out into their apostasy much later, even during the intermediate period of the Church.

CHAP. V. — CHRIST AND HIS APOSTLES, WITHOUT ANY FRAUD, DECEPTION, OR HYPOCRISY, PREACHED THAT ONE GOD, THE FATHER, WAS THE FOUNDER OF ALL THINGS. THEY DID NOT ACCOMMODATE THEIR DOCTRINETO THE PREPOSSESSIONS OF THEIR HEARERS.

1. Since, therefore, the tradition from the apostles does thus exist in the Church, and is permanent among us, let us revert to the Scrip–rural proof furnished by those apostles

who did also write the Gospel, in which they recorded the doctrine regarding God, pointing out that our Lord Jesus Christ is the truth,(7) and that no lie is in Him. As also David says, prophesying His birth from a virgin, and the resurrection from the dead, "Truth has sprung out of the earth."(8) The apostles, likewise, being disciples of the truth, are above all falsehood; for a lie has no fellowship with the truth, just as darkness has none with light, but the presence of the one shuts out that of the other. Our Lord, therefore, being the truth, did not speak lies; and whom He knew to have taken origin from a de−feet, He never would have acknowledged as God, even the God of all, the Supreme King, too, and His own Father, an imperfect being as a perfect one, an animal one as a spiritual, Him who was without the Pleroma as Him who was within it. Neither did His disciples make mention of any other God, or term any other Lord, except Him, who was truly the God and Lord of all, as these most vain sophists affirm that the apostles did with hypocrisy frame their doctrine according to the capacity of their hearers, and gave answers after the opinions of their questioners,—fabling blind things for the blind, according to their blindness; for the dull according to their dulness; for those in error according to their error. And to those who imagined that the Demiurge alone was God, they preached him; but to those who are capable of comprehending the unnameable Father, they did declare the unspeakable mystery through parables and enigmas: so that the Lord and the apostles exercised the office of teacher not to further the cause of truth, but even in hypocrisy, and as each individual was able to receive it!

5. Such [a line of conduct] belongs not to those who heal, or who give life: it is rather that of those bringing on diseases, and increasing ignorance; and much more true than these men shall the law be found, which pronounces every one accursed who sends the blind man astray in the way. For the apostles, who were commissioned to find out the wanderers, and to be for sight to those who saw not, and medicine to the weak, certainly did not address them in accordance with their opinion at the time, but according to revealed truth. For no persons of any kind would act properly, if they should advise blind men, just about to fall over a precipice, to continue their most dangerous path, as if it were the right one, and as if they might go on in safety. Or what medical man, anxious to heal a sick person, would prescribe in accordance with the patient's whims, and not according to the requisite medicine? But that the Lord came as the physician of the sick, He does Himself declare saying, "They that are whole need not a physician, but they that are sick; I came not to call the righteous, but sinners to repentance."(1) How then shall the sick be strengthened, or how shall sinners come to repentance? Is it by persevering in the very same courses? or, on the contrary, is it by undergoing a great change and

reversal of their former mode of living, by which they have brought upon themselves no slight amount of sickness, and many sins? But ignorance, the mother of all these, is driven out by knowledge. Wherefore the Lord used to impart knowledge to His disciples, by which also it was His practice to heal those who were suffering, and to keep back sinners from sin. He therefore did not address them in accordance with their pristine notions, nor did He reply to them in harmony with the opinion of His questioners,

but according to the doctrine leading to salvation, without hypocrisy or respect of person.

3. This is also made clear from the words of the Lord, who did truly reveal the Son of God to those of the circumcision—Him who had been foretold as Christ by the prophets; that is, He set Himself forth, who had restored liberty

men, and bestowed on them the inheritance to incorruption And again, the apostles taught the Gentiles that they should leave vain stocks and stones, which they imagined to be gods, and worship the true God, who had created and made all the human family, and, by means of His creation, did nourish, increase, strengthen, and preserve them in being; and that they might look for His Son Jesus Christ, who redeemed us from apostasy with His own blood, so that we should also be a sanctified people, — who shall also descend from heaven in His Father's power, and pass judgment upon all, and who shall freely give the good things of God to those who shall have kept His commandments. He, appearing in these last times, the chief cornerstone, has gathered into one, and united those that were far off and those that were near;(2) that is, the circumcision and the uncircumcision, enlarging Japhet, and placing him in the dwelling of Shem.(3)

CHAP. VI — THE HOLY GHOST, THROUGHOUT THE OLD TESTAMENT SCRIPTURES, MADE MENTION OF NO OTHER GOD OR LORD, SAVE HIM WHO IS THE TRUE GOD.

1. Therefore neither would the Lord, nor the Holy Spirit, nor the apostles, have ever named as God, definitely and absolutely, him who was not God, unless he were truly God; nor would they have named any one in his own person Lord, except God the Father ruling over all, and His Son who has received dominion from His Father over all creation, as this passage has it: "The LORD said unto my Lord, Sit Thou at my right hand, until I

make Thine enemies Thy footstool."(4) Here the [Scripture] represents to us the Father addressing the Son; He who gave Him the inheritance of the heathen, and subjected to Him all His enemies. Since, therefore, the Father is truly Lord, and the Son truly Lord, the Holy Spirit has fitly designated them by the title of Lord. And again, referring to the destruction of the Sodomites, the Scripture says, "Then the LORD rained upon Sodom and upon Gomorrah fire and brimstone from the LORD out of heaven."(5) For it here points out that the Son, who had also been talking with Abraham, had received power to judge the Sodomites for their wickedness. And this [text following] does declare the same truth: "Thy throne, O God; is for ever and ever; the sceptre of Thy kingdom is a right sceptre. Thou hast loved righteousness, and hated iniquity: therefore God, Thy God, hath anointed Thee."(1) For the Spirit designates both [of them] by the name, of God — both Him who is anointed as Son, and Him who does anoint, that is, the Father. And again: "God stood in the congregation of the gods, He judges among the gods."(2) He [here] refers to the Father and the Son, and those who have received the adoption; but these are the Church. For she is the synagogue of God, which God—that is, the Son Himself—has gathered by Himself. Of whom He again speaks: "The God of gods, the Lord hath spoken, and hath called the earth."(3) Who is meant by God? He of whom He has said, "God shall come openly, our God, and shall not keep silence; "(4) that is, the Son, who came manifested to men who said, "I have openly appeared to those who seek Me not."(5) But of what gods [does he speak]? [Of those] to whom He says, "I have said, Ye are gods, and all sons of the Most High."(6) To those, no doubt, who have received the grace of the "adoption, by which we cry, Abba Father."(7)

2. Wherefore, as I have already stated, no other is named as God, or is called Lord, except Him who is God and Lord of all, who also said to Moses, "I AM THAT I AM. And thus shalt thou say to the children of Israel: He who is, hath sent me unto you;"(8) and His Son Jesus Christ our Lord, who makes those that believe in His name the sons of God. And again, when the Son speaks to Moses, He says, "I am come down to deliver this people."(9) For it is He who descended and ascended for the salvation of men. Therefore God has been declared through the Son, who is in the Father, and has the Father in Himself — He who is, the Father bearing witness to the Son, and the Son announcing the Father. — As also Esaias says, "I too am witness," he declares, "saith the LORD God, and the Son whom I have chosen, that ye may know, and believe, and understand that I am."(10)

3. When, however, the Scripture terms them [gods] which are no gods, it does not, as I have already remarked, declare them as gods in every sense, but with a certain addition and signification, by which they are shown to be no gods at all. As with David: "The gods of the heathen

are idols of demons;"(11) and, "Ye shall not follow other gods"(12) For in that he says "the gods of the heathen"— but the heathen are ignorant of the true God — and calls them "other gods," he bars their claim [to be looked upon] as gods at all. But as to what they are in their own person, he speaks concerning them; "for they are," he says, "the idols of demons." And Esaias: "Let them be confounded, all who blaspheme God, and carve useless things;(13) even I am witness, saith God."(14) He removes them from [the category of] gods, but he makes use of the word alone, for this [purpose], that we may know of whom he speaks. Jeremiah also says the same: "The gods that have not made the heavens and earth, let them perish from the earth which is under the heaven."(15) For, from the fact of his having subjoined their destruction, he shows them to be no gods at all. Elias, too, when all Israel was assembled at Mount Carmel, wishing to turn them from idolatry, says to them, "How long halt ye between two opinions?(16) If the LORD be God,(17) follow Him."(18) And again, at the burnt-offering, he thus addresses the idolatrous priests: "Ye shall call upon the name of your gods, and I will call on the name of the LORD my God; and the Lord that will hearken by fire,(19) He is God." Now, from the fact of the prophet having said these words, he proves that these gods which were reputed so among those men, are no gods at all. He directed them to that God upon whom he believed, and who was truly God; whom invoking, he exclaimed, "LORD God of Abraham, God of Isaac, and God of Jacob, hear me to-day, and let all this people know that Thou art the God of Israel."(20)

4. Wherefore I do also call upon thee, LORD God of Abraham, and God of Isaac, and God of Jacob and Israel, who art the Father of our Lord Jesus Christ, the God who, through the abundance of Thy mercy, hast had a favour towards us, that we should know Thee, who hast made heaven and earth, who rulest over all, who art the only and the true God, above whom there is none other God; grant, by our Lord Jesus Christ, the governing power of the Holy Spirit; give to every reader of this book to know Thee, that Thou art God alone, to be strengthened in Thee, and to avoid every heretical, and godless, and impious doctrine. 5. And the Apostle Paul also, saying, "For though ye have served them which are no gods; ye now know God, or rather, are known of God,"(1) has made a separation between those that were not [gods] and Him who is God. And again, speaking

of Antichrist, he says, "who opposeth and exalteth himself above all that is called God, or that is worshipped."(2) He points out here those who are called gods, by such as know not God, that is, idols. For the Father of all is called God, and is so; and Antichrist shall be lifted up, not above Him, but above those which are indeed called gods, but are not. And Paul himself says that this is true: "We know that an idol is nothing, and that there is none other God but one. For though there be that are called gods, whether in heaven or in earth; yet to us there is but one God, the Father, of whom are all things, and we through Him; and one Lord Jesus Christ, by whom are all things, and we by Him."(3) For he has made a distinction, and separated those which are indeed called gods, but which are none, from the one God the Father, from whom are all things, and, he has confessed in the most decided manner in his own person, one Lord Jesus Christ. But in this [clause], "whether in heaven or in earth," he does not speak of the formers of the world, as these [teachers] expound it; but his meaning is similar to that of Moses, when it is said, "Thou shalt not make to thyself any image for God, of whatsoever things are in heaven above, whatsoever in the earth beneath, and whatsoever in the waters under the earth."(4) And he does thus explain what are meant by the things in heaven: "Lest when," he says, "looking towards heaven, and observing the sun, and the moon, and the stars, and all the ornament of heaven, falling into error, thou shouldest adore and serve them."(5) And Moses himself, being a man of God, was indeed given as a god before Pharaoh;(6) but he is not properly termed Lord, nor is called God by the prophets, but is spoken of by the Spirit as "Moses, the faithful minister and servant of God,"(7) which also he was.

CHAP. VII. — REPLY TO AN OBJECTION FOUNDED ON THE WORDS OF ST. PAUL (2 Cor. IV. 5). ST. PAUL OCCASIONALLY USES WORDS NOT IN THEIR GRAMMATICAL, SEQUENCE.

1. As to their affirming that Paul said plainly in the Second [Epistle] to the Corinthians, "In whom the god of this world hath blinded the minds of them that believe not,"(8) and maintain–

ing that there is indeed one god of this world, but another who is beyond all principality, and beginning, and power, we are not to blame if they, who give out that they do themselves know mysteries beyond God, know not how to read Paul. For if any one read the passage thus—according to Paul's custom, as I show elsewhere, and by many examples, that he uses transposition of words —"In whom God," then pointing it off, and making a slight interval, and at the same time read also the rest [of the sentence] in one [clause], "hath blinded the minds of them of this world that believe not," he shall find out the true [sense]; that it is contained in the expression, "God hath blinded the minds of the unbelievers of this world." And this is shown by means of the little interval [between the clause]. For Paul does not say, "the God of this world," as if recognising any other beyond Him; but he confessed God as indeed God. And he says, "the unbelievers of this world," because they shall not inherit the future age of incorruption. I shall show from Paul himself, how it is that God has blinded the minds of them that believe not, in the course of this work, that we may not just at present distract our mind from the matter in hand, [by wandering] at large.

2. From many other instances also, we may discover that the apostle frequently uses a transposed order in his sentences, due to the rapidity of his discourses, and the impetus of the Spirit which is in him. An example occurs in the [Epistle] to the Galatians, where he expresses himself as follows: "Wherefore then the law of works?(9) It was added, until the seed should come to whom the promise was made; [and it was] ordained by angels in the hand of a Mediator."(10) For the order of the words runs thus: "Wherefore then the law of works? Ordained by angels in the hand of a Mediator, it was added until the seed should come to whom the promise was made," — man thus asking the question, and the Spirit making answer. And again, in the Second to the Thessalonians, speaking of Antichrist, he says, "And then shall that wicked be revealed, whom the Lord Jesus Christ(11) shall slay with the Spirit of His mouth, and shall destroy him(11) with the presence of his coming; [even him] whose coming is after the working of Satan, with all power, and signs, and lying wonders."(12) Now in these [sentences] the order of the words is this: "And then shall be revealed that wicked, whose coming is after the working of Satan, with all power, and signs, and lying wonders, whom the Lord Jesus shall slay with the Spirit of His mouth, and shall destroy with the presence of His coming." For he does not mean that the coming of the Lord is after the working of Satan; but the coming of the wicked one, whom we also call Antichrist. If, then, one does not attend to the [proper] reading [of the passage], and if he do not exhibit the intervals of breathing as they occur, there shall be not only incongruities, but also, when reading, he will utter blasphemy, as if the advent of the Lord could take place according to the working of Satan. So therefore, in such passages, the hyperbaton must be exhibited by the reading, and the apostle's meaning following on, preserved; and thus we do not read in that passage, "the god of this world," but, "God," whom we do truly call God; and we hear [it

declared of] the unbelieving and the blinded of this world, that they shall not inherit the world of life which is to come.

CHAP. VIII. — ANSWER TO AN OBJECTION, ARISING FROM THE WORDS OF CHRIST (MATT. VI. 24). GOD ALONE IS TO BE REALLY CALLED GOD AND LORD, FOR HE IS WITHOUT BEGINNING AND END.

1. This calumny, then, of these men, having been quashed, it is clearly proved that neither the prophets nor the apostles did ever name another God, or call [him] Lord, except the true and only God. Much more [would this be the case with regard to] the Lord Himself, who did also direct us to "render unto Caesar the things that are Caesar's, and to God the things that are God's;"(1) naming indeed Caesar as Caesar, but confessing God as God. In like manner also, that [text] which says, "Ye cannot serve two masters,"(2) He does Himself interpret, saying, "Ye cannot serve God and mammon;" acknowledging God indeed as God, but mentioning mammon, a thing having also an existence. He does not call mammon Lord when He says, "Ye cannot serve two masters;" but He teaches His disciples who serve God, not to be subject to mammon, nor to be ruled by it. For He says, "He that committeth sin is the slave of sin."(3) Inasmuch, then, as He terms those "the slaves of sin" who serve sin, but does not certainly call sin itself God, thus also He terms those who serve mammon "the slaves of mammon," not calling mammon God. For mammon is, according to the Jewish language, which the Samaritans do also use, a covetous man, and one who wishes to have more than he ought to have. But according to the Hebrew, it is by the addition of a syllable (adjunctive)

called Mamuel,(4) and signifies gulosum, that is, one whose gullet is insatiable. Therefore, according to both these things which are indicated, we cannot serve God and mammon.

2. But also, when He spoke of the devil as strong, not absolutely so, but as in comparison with us, the Lord showed Himself under every aspect and truly to be the strong man, saying that one can in no other way "spoil the goods of a strong man, if he do not first bind the strong man himself, and then he will spoil his house."(5) Now we were the vessels and the house of this [strong man] when we were in a state of apostasy; for he put us to whatever use he pleased, and the unclean spirit dwelt within us. For he was not

strong, as opposed to Him who bound him, and spoiled his house; but as against those persons who were his tools, inasmuch as he caused their thought to wander away from God: these did the Lord snatch from his grasp. As also Jeremiah declares, "The LORD hath redeemed Jacob, and has snatched him from the hand of him that was stronger than he."(6) If, then, he had not pointed out Him who binds and spoils his goods, but had merely spoken of him as being strong, the strong man should have been unconquered. But he also subjoined Him who obtains and retains possession; for he holds who binds, but he is held who is bound. And this he did without any comparison, so that, apostate slave as he was, he might not be compared to the Lord: for not he alone, but not one of created and subject things, shall ever be compared to the Word of God, by whom all things were made, who is our Lord Jesus Christ.

3. For that all things, whether Angels, or Archangels, or Thrones, or Dominions, were both established and created by Him who is God over all, through His Word, John has thus pointed out. For when he had spoken of the Word of God as having been in the Father, he added, "All things were made by Him, and without Him was not anything made."(7) David also, when he had enumerated [His] praises, subjoins by name all things whatsoever I have mentioned, both the heavens and all the powers therein: "For He commanded, and they were created; He spake, and they were made." Whom, therefore, did He command? The Word, no doubt, "by whom," he says, "the heavens were established, and all their power by the breath of His mouth."(8) But that He did Him– self make all things freely, and as He pleased, again David says, "But our God is in the heavens above, and in the earth; He hath made all things whatsoever He pleased."(1) But the things established are distinct from Him who has established them, and what have been made from Him who has made them. For He is Himself uncreated, both without beginning and end, and lacking nothing. He is Himself sufficient for Himself; and still further, He grants to all others this very thing, existence; but the things which have been made by Him have received a beginning. But whatever things had a beginning, and are liable to dissolution, and are subject to and stand in need of Him who made them, must necessarily in all respects have a different term [applied to them], even by those who have but a moderate capacity for discerning such things; so that He indeed who made all things can alone, together with His Word, properly be termed God and Lord: but the things which have been made cannot have this term applied to them, neither should they justly assume that appellation which belongs to the Creator.

CHAP. IX. — ONE AND THE SAME GOD, THE CREATOR OF HEAVEN AND EARTH, IS HE WHOM THE PROPHETS FORETOLD, AND WHO WAS DECLARED BY THE GOSPEL. PROOF OF THIS, AT THE OUTSET, FROM ST. MATTHEW'S GOSPEL.

1. This, therefore, having been clearly demonstrated here (and it shall yet be so still more clearly), that neither the prophets, nor the apostles, nor the Lord Christ in His own person, did acknowledge any other Lord or God, but the God and Lord supreme: the prophets and the apostles confessing the Father and the Son; but naming no other as God, and confessing no other as Lord: and the Lord Himself handing down to His disciples, that He, the Father, is the only God and Lord, who alone is God and ruler of all; — it is incumbent on us to follow, if we are their disciples indeed, their testimonies to this effect. For Matthew the apostle — knowing, as one and the same God, Him who had given promise to Abraham, that He would make his seed as the stars of heaven,(2) and Him who, by His Son Christ Jesus, has called us to the knowledge of Himself, from the worship of stones, so that those who were not a people were made a people, and she beloved who was not beloved(3) —declares that John, when preparing the way for Christ, said to those who were boasting of their relationship [to Abraham] according to the flesh, but who had their mind tinged and stuffed with all manner of evil, preaching that repentance which should call them back from their evil

doings, said, "O generation of vipers, who hath shown you to flee from the wrath to come? Bring forth therefore fruit meet for repentance. And think not to say within yourselves, We have Abraham [to our] father: for I say unto you, that God is able of these stones to raise up children unto Abraham."(4) He preached to them, therefore, the repentance from wickedness, but he did not declare to them another God, besides Him who made the promise to Abraham; he, the forerunner of Christ, of whom Matthew again says, and Luke likewise, "For this is he that was spoken of from the Lord by the prophet, The voice of one crying in the wilderness, Prepare ye the way of the Lord, make straight the paths of our God. Every valley shall be filled, and every mountain and hill brought low; and the crooked shall be made straight, and the rough into smooth ways; and all flesh shall see the salvation of God."(5) There is therefore one and the same God, the Father of our Lord, who also promised, through the prophets, that He would send His forerunner; and His salvation — that is, His Word — He caused to be made visible to all flesh, [the Word] Himself being made incarnate, that in all things their King might become manifest. For it is necessary that those [beings] which are judged do see the judge, and know Him from whom they receive judgment; and it is also proper, that those which follow on to glory should know Him who bestows upon them the gift of glory.

2. Then again Matthew, when speaking of the angel, says, "The angel of the Lord appeared to Joseph in sleep."(6) Of what Lord he does himself interpret: "That it may be fulfilled which was spoken of the Lord by the prophet, Out of Egypt have I called my son."(7) "Behold, a virgin shall conceive, and shall bring forth a son, and they shall call his name Emmanuel; which is, being interpreted, God with us."(8) David likewise speaks of Him who, from the virgin, is Emmanuel: "Turn not away the face of Thine anointed. The LORD hath sworn a truth to David, and will not turn from him. Of the fruit of thy body will I set upon thy seat."(9) And again: "In Judea is God known; His place has been made in peace, and His dwelling in Zion."(10) Therefore there is one and the same God, who was proclaimed by the prophets and announced by the Gospel; and His Son, who was of the fruit of David's body, that is, of the virgin of [the house of] David, and Emmanuel; whose star also Balaam thus prophesied: "There shall come a star out of Jacob, and a leader shall rise in Israel."(1) But Matthew says that the Magi, coming from the east, exclaimed "For we have seen His star in the east, and are come to worship Him;"(2) and that, having been led by the star into the house of Jacob to Emmanuel, they showed, by these gifts which they offered, who it was that was worshipped; myrrh, because it was He who should die and be buried for the mortal human met; gold, because He was a King, "of whose kingdom is no end;"(3) and frankincense, because He was God, who also "was made known in Judea,"(4) and was "declared to those who sought Him not."(5)

3. And then, [speaking of His] baptism, Matthew says, "The heavens were opened, and He saw the Spirit of God, as a dove, coming upon Him: and lo a voice from heaven, saying, This is my beloved Son, in whom I am well pleased."(6) For Christ did not at that time descend upon Jesus, neither was Christ one and Jesus another: but the Word of God—who is the Saviour of all, and the ruler of heaven and earth, who is Jesus, as I have already pointed out, who did also take upon Him flesh, and was anointed by the Spirit from the Father—was made Jesus Christ, as Esaias also says, "There shall come forth a rod from the root of Jesse, and a flower shall rise from his root; and the Spirit of God shall rest upon Him: the spirit of wisdom and understanding, the spirit of counsel and

might, the spirit of knowledge and piety, and the spirit of the fear of God, shall fill Him. He shall not judge according to glory,(7) nor reprove after the manner of speech; but He shall dispense judgment to the humble man, and reprove the haughty ones of the earth."(8) And again Esaias, pointing out beforehand His unction, and the reason why he was anointed, does himself say, "The Spirit of God is upon Me, because He hath anointed Me: He hath sent Me to preach the Gospel to the lowly, to heal the broken up in heart, to proclaim liberty to the captives, and sight to the blind; to announce the acceptable year of the Lord, and the day of vengeance; to comfort all that mourn."(9) For inasmuch as the Word of God was man from the root of Jesse, and son of Abraham, in this respect did the Spirit of God rest upon Him, and anoint Him to preach the Gospel to the lowly. But inasmuch as He was God, He did not judge according to

glory, nor reprove after the manner of speech. For "He needed not that any should testify to Him of man,(10) for He Himself knew what was in man."(11) For He called all men that mourn; and granting forgiveness to those who had been led into captivity by their sins, He loosed them from their chains, of whom Solomon says, "Every one shall be holden with the cords of his own sins."(12) Therefore did the Spirit of God descend upon Him, [the Spirit] of Him who had promised by the prophets that He would anoint Him, so that we, receiving from the abundance of His unction, might be saved. Such, then, [is the witness] of Matthew.

CHAP. X.—PROOFS OF THE FOREGOING, DRAWN FROM THE GOSPELS OF MARK AND LUKE.

1. Luke also, the follower and disciple of the apostles, referring to Zacharias and Elisabeth, from whom, according to promise, John was born, says: "And they were both righteous before God, walking in all the commandments and ordinances of the Lord blameless."(13) And again, speaking of Zacharias: "And it came to pass, that while he executed the priest's office before God in the order of his course, according to the custom of the priest's office, his lot was to burn incense; "(14) and he came to sacrifice, "entering into the temple of the Lord."(15) Whose angel Gabriel, also, who stands prominently in the presence of the Lord, simply, absolutely, and decidedly confessed in his own person as God and Lord, Him who had chosen Jerusalem, and had instituted the sacerdotal office. For he knew of none other above Him; since, if he had been in possession of the knowledge of any other more perfect God and Lord besides Him, he surely would

never—as I have already shown—have confessed Him, whom he knew to be the fruit of a defect, as absolutely and altogether God and Lord. And then, speaking of John, he thus says: "For he shall be great in the sight of the Lord, and many of the children of Israel shall he turn to the Lord their God. And he shall go before Him in the spirit and power of Elias, to make ready a people prepared for the Lord."(16) For whom, then, did he prepare the people, and in the sight of what Lord was he made great? Truly of Him who said that John had something even "more than a prophet,"(17) and that "among those born of women none is greater than John the Baptist;" who did also make the people ready for the Lord's advent, warning his fellow-servants, and preaching to them repentance, that they might receive remission from the Lord when He should be present, having been convened to Him, from whom they had been alienated because of sins and transgressions. As also David says, "The alienated are sinners from the womb: they go astray as soon as they are born."(1) And it was on account of this that he, turning them to their Lord, prepared, in the spirit and power of Elias, a perfect people for the Lord.

2. And again, speaking in reference to the angel, he says: "But at that time the angel Gabriel was sent from God, who did also say to the virgin, Fear not, Mary; for thou hast found favour with God."(2) And he says concerning the Lord: "He shall be great, and shall be called the Son of the Highest: and the Lord God shall give unto Him the throne of His father David: and He shall reign over the house of Jacob for ever; and of His kingdom there shall be no end."(3) For who else is there who can reign uninterruptedly over the house of Jacob for ever, except Jesus Christ our Lord, the Son of the Most High God, who promised by the law and the prophets that He would make His salvation visible to all flesh; so that He would become the Son of man for this purpose, that man also might become the son of God? And Mary, exulting because of this, cried out, prophesying on behalf of the Church, "My soul doth magnify the Lord, and my spirit hath rejoiced in God my Saviour. For He hath taken up His child Israel, in remembrance of His mercy, as He spake to our fathers, Abraham, and his seed for ever."(4) By these and such like [passages] the Gospel points out that it was God who spake to the fathers; that it was He who, by Moses, instituted the legal dispensation, by which giving of the law we know that He spake to the fathers. This same God,. after His great goodness, poured His compassion upon us, through which compassion "the Day-spring from on high hath looked upon us, and appeared to those who sat in darkness and the shadow of death, and has guided our feet into the way of peace;"(5) as Zacharias also, recovering from the state of dumbness which he had suffered on account of unbelief, having been filled with a new spirit, did bless God in a new manner. For all things had entered upon a new phase, the

Word arranging after a new manner the advent in the flesh, that He might win back(6) to God that human nature (hominem) which had departed from God; and therefore men were taught to worship God after a new fashion, but not another god, because in truth there is but "one God, who justifieth the circumcision by

faith, and the uncircumcision through faith."(7) But Zacharias prophesying, exclaimed, "Blessed be the Lord God of Israel; for He hath visited and redeemed His people, and hath raised up an horn of salvation for us in the house of His servant David; as He spake by the mouth of His holy prophets, which have been since the world begun; salvation from our enemies, and from the hand of all that hate us; to perform the mercy [promised] to our fathers, and to remember His holy covenant, the oath which He sware to our father Abraham, that He would grant unto us, that we, being delivered out of the hand of our enemies, might serve Him without fear, in holiness and righteousness before Him, all our days."(8) Then he says to John: "And thou, child, shalt be called the prophet of the Highest: for thou shalt go before the face of the Lord to prepare HiS ways; to give knowledge of salvation to His people, for the remission of their sins."(9) For this is the knowledge of salvation which was wanting to them, that of the Son of God, which John made known, saying, "Behold the Lamb of God, who taketh away the sin of the world. This is He of whom I said, After me cometh a man who was made before me;(10) because He was prior to me: and of His fulness have all we received."(11) This, therefore, was the knowledge of salvation; but [it did not consist in] another God, nor another Father, nor Bythus, nor the Pleroma of thirty Aeons, nor the Mother of the (lower) Ogdoad: but the knowledge of salvation was the knowledge of the Son of God, who is both called and actually is, salvation, and Saviour, and salutary. Salvation, indeed, as follows: "I have waited for Thy salvation, O Lord."(12) And then again, Saviour: "Behold my God, my Saviour, I will put my trust in Him."(13) But as bringing salvation, thus: "God hath made known His salvation (salutare) in the sight of the heathen."(14) For He is indeed Saviour, as being the Son and Word of God; but salutary, since [He is] Spirit; for he says: "The Spirit of our countenance, Christ the Lord."(15) But salvation, as being flesh: for "the Word was made flesh, and dwelt among us."(16) This knowledge of salvation, therefore, John did impart to those repenting, and believing in the Lamb of God, who taketh away the sin of the world. 3. And the angel of the Lord, he says, appeared to the shepherds, proclaiming joy to them: "For(1) there is born in the house of David, a Saviour, which is Christ the Lord. Then [appeared] a multitude of the heavenly host, praising God, and saying, Glory in the highest to God, and on earth peace, to men of good will." (2) The falsely-called Gnostics say that these angels came from the Ogdoad, and made manifest the descent of the superior Christ. But they are again in error, when saying that the Christ and Saviour from above was not born, but that also, after the baptism of the dispensational Jesus, he, [the Christ of the Pleroma,] descended upon him as a dove. Therefore, according to these men, the angels of the Ogdoad lied, when they said, "For unto you is born this day a Saviour, who is Christ the Lord, in the city of David." For neither was Christ nor the Saviour born at that time, by their account; but it was he, the dispensational Jesus, who is of the framer of the world, the [Demiurge], and upon whom, after his baptism, that is, after [the lapse of] thirty years, they maintain the Saviour from above descended. But why did [the angels] add, "in the city of David," if they did not proclaim the glad tidings of the fulfilment of God's promise made to David, that from the fruit of his body there should be an eternal King? For the Framer [Demiurge] of the entire universe made promise to David, as David himself declares: "My help is from God, who made heaven and earth;"(3) and again: "In His hand are the ends of the earth, and the heights of the mountains are His. For the sea is His, and He did Himself make it; and His hands founded the dry land. Come ye, let us worship and fall down before Him, and weep in the presence of the Lord who made us; for He is the Lord our God."(4) The Holy Spirit evidently thus declares by David to those hearing him, that there shall be those who despise Him who formed us, and who is God alone. Wherefore he also uttered the foregoing words, meaning to say: See that ye do not err; besides or above Him there is no other God, to whom ye should rather stretch out [your hands], thus rendering us pious and grateful towards Him who made, established, and [still] nourishes us. What, then, shall happen to those who have been the authors of so much blasphemy against their Creator ? This identical truth was also what the

angels [proclaimed]. For when they exclaim, "Glory to God in the highest, and in earth peace," they have glorified with these. words Him who is the Creator of the highest, that is, of super–celestial things, and the Founder of everything on earth: who has sent to His own handiwork, that is, to men, the blessing of His salvation from heaven. Wherefore he adds: "The shepherds returned, glorifying God for all which they had heard and seen, as it was told unto them."(5) For the Israelitish shepherds did not glorify another god, but Him who had been announced by the law and the prophets, the Maker of all things, whom also the angels glorified. But if the angels who were from the Ogdoad were accustomed to glorify any other, different from Him whom the shepherds [adored], these angels from the Ogdoad brought to them error and not truth.

4. And still further does Luke say in reference to the Lord: "When the days of purification were accomplished, they brought Him up to Jerusalem, to present Him before the Lord, as it is written in the law of the Lord, That every male opening the womb shall be called holy to the Lord; and that they should offer a sacrifice, as it is said in the law of the Lord, a pair of turtle–doves, or two young pigeons:"(6) in his own person most clearly calling Him Lord, who appointed the legal dispensation. But "Simeon," he also says, "blessed God, and said, Lord, now lettest Thou Thy servant depart in peace; for mine eyes have seen Thy salvation, which Thou hast prepared before the face of all people; a light for the revelation of the Gentiles, and the glory of Thy people Israel."(7) And "Anna"(8) also, "the prophetess," he says, in like manner glorified God when she saw Christ, "and spake of Him to all them who were looking for the redemption of Jerusalem."(9) Now by all these one God is shown forth, revealing to men the new dispensation of liberty, the covenant, through the new advent of His Son.

5. Wherefore also Mark, the interpreter and follower of Peter, does thus commence his Gospel narrative: "The beginning of the Gospel of Jesus Christ, the Son of God; as it is written in the prophets, Behold, I send My messenger before Thy face, which shall prepare Thy way.(10) The voice of one crying in the wilderness, Prepare ye the way of the Lord, make the paths straight before our God." Plainly does the commencement of the Gospel quote the words of the holy prophets, and point out Him at once, whom they confessed as God and Lord; Him, the Father of our Lord Jesus Christ, who had also made promise to Him, that He would send His messenger before His face, who was John, crying in the wilderness, in "the spirit and power of Elias,"(1)"Prepare ye the way of me Lord, make straight paths before our God." For the prophets did not announce one and mother God, but one and the same; under rations aspects, however, and many titles. For varied and rich in attribute is the Father, as I have already shown in the book preceding(2) this; and I shall show [the same truth] from the prophets themselves in the further course of this work. Also, towards the conclusion of his Gospel, Mark says: "So then, after the Lord Jesus had spoken to them, He was received up into heaven, and sitteth on the right hand of God;"(3) confirming what had been spoken by the prophet: "The LORD said to my Lord, Sit Thou on My right hand, until I make Thy foes Thy footstool."(4) Thus God and the Father are truly one and the same; He who was announced by the prophets, and handed down by the true Gospel; whom we Christians worship and love with the whole heart, as the Maker of heaven and earth, and of all things therein.

CHAP. XI—PROOFS IN CONTINUATION, EXTRACTED FROM ST. JOHN'S GOSPEL. THE GOSPELS ARE FOUR IN NUMBER, NEITHER MORE NOR LESS. MYSTIC REASONS FOR THIS.

1. John, the disciple of the Lord, preaches this faith, and seeks, by the proclamation of the Gospel, to remove that error which by Cerinthus had been disseminated among men, and a long time previously by those termed Nicolaitans, who are an offset of that "knowledge" falsely so called, that he might confound them, and persuade them that there is but one God, who made all things by His Word; and not, as they allege, that the Creator was one, but the Father of the Lord another; and that the Son of the Creator was, forsooth, one, but the Christ from above another, who also continued impossible, descending upon Jesus, the Son of the Creator, and flew back again into His Pleroma; and that Monogenes was the beginning, but Logos was the true son of Monogenes; and that this creation to which we belong was not made by the primary God, but by some power lying far below Him, and shut off from communion with the things invisible and ineffable. The disciple of the Lord

therefore desiring to put an end to all such doctrines, and to establish the rule of truth in the Church, that there is one Almighty God, who made all things by His Word, both visible and invisible; showing at the same time, that by the Word, through whom God made the creation, He also bestowed salvation on the men included in the creation; thus commenced His teaching in the Gospel: "In the beginning was the Word, and the Word was with God, and the WOrd was God. The same was in the beginning with God. All things were made by Him, and without Him was nothing made.(5) What was made was life in Him, and the life was the light of men. And the light shineth in darkness, and the darkness comprehended it not."(6) "All things," he says, "were made by Him;" therefore in "all things" this creation of ours is [included], for we cannot concede to these men that [the words] "all things" are spoken in reference to those within their Pleroma. For if their Pleroma do indeed contain these, this creation, as being such, is not outside, as I have demonstrated in the preceding book;(7) but if they are outside the Pleroma, which indeed appeared impossible, it follows, in that case, that their Pleroma cannot be "all things:" therefore this vast creation is not outside [the Pleroma].

2. John, however, does himself put this matter beyond all controversy on our part, when he says, "He was in this world, and the world was made by Him, and the world knew Him not. He came unto His own [things], and His own [people] received Him not."(8) But according to Marcion, and those like him, neither was the world made by Him; nor did He come to His own things, but to those of another. And, according to certain of the Gnostics, this world was made by angels, and not by the Word of God. But according to the followers of Valentinus, the world was not made by Him, but by the Demiurge. For he (Soter) caused such similitudes to be made, after the pattern of things above, as they allege; but the Demiurge accomplished the work of creation. For they say that he, the Lord and Creator of the plan of creation, by whom they hold that this world was made, was produced from the Mother; while the Gospel affirms plainly, that by the Word, which was in the beginning with God, all things were made, which Word, he says, "was made flesh, and dwelt among us."(9)

3. But, according to these men, neither was the Word made flesh, nor Christ, nor the Saviour (Soter), who was produced from [the joint con– tributions of] all [the Aeons]. For they will have it, that the Word and Christ never came into this world; that the Saviour, too, never became incarnate, nor suffered, but that He descended like a dove upon the dispensational Jesus; and that, as soon as He had declared the unknown Father, He did again ascend into the Pleroma. Some, however, make the assertion, that this dispensational Jesus did become incarnate, and suffered, whom they represent as having passed through Mary just as water through a tube; but others allege him to be the Son of the Demiurge, upon whom the dispensational Jesus descended; while others, again, say that Jesus was born from Joseph and Mary, and that the Christ from above descended upon him, being without flesh, and impassible. But according to the opinion of no one of the heretics was the Word of God made flesh. For if any one carefully examines the systems of them all, he will find that the Word of God is brought in by all of them as not having become incarnate (sine carne) and impassible, as is also the Christ from above. Others consider Him to have been manifested as a transfigured man; but they maintain Him to have been neither born nor to have become incarnate; whilst others [hold] that He did not assume a human form at all, but that, as a dove, He did descend upon that Jesus who was born from Mary. Therefore the Lord's disciple, pointing them all out as false witnesses, says, "And the Word was made flesh, and dwelt among us."(1)

4. And that we may not have to ask, Of what God was the Word made flesh ? he does himself previously teach us, saying, "There was a man sent from God, whose name was

John. The same came as a witness, that he might bear witness of that Light. He was not that Light, but [came] that he might testify of the Light."(2) By what God, then, was John, the forerunner, who testifies of the Light, sent [into the world]? Truly it was by Him, of whom Gabriel is the angel, who also announced the glad tidings of his birth: [that God] who also had promised by the prophets that He would send His messenger before the face of His Son,(3) who should prepare His way, that is, that he should bear witness of that Light in the spirit and power of Elias.(4) But, again, of what God was Elias the servant and the prophet? Of Him who made heaven and earth,(5) as he does himself confess. John, therefore, having been sent by the founder and maker of this world, how could he testify of that Light, which came down from things unspeakable

and invisible? For all the heretics have decided that the Demiurge was ignorant of that Power above him, whose witness and herald John is found to be. Wherefore the Lord said that He deemed him "more than a prophet."(6) For all the other prophets preached the advent of the paternal Light, and desired to be worthy of seeing Him whom they preached; but John did both announce [the advent] beforehand, in a like manner as did the others, and actually saw Him when He came, and pointed Him out, and persuaded many to believe on Him, so that he did himself hold the place of both prophet and apostle. For this is to be more than a prophet, because, "first apostles, secondarily prophets; "(7) but all things from one and the same God Himself.

5. That wine,(8) which was produced by God in a vineyard, and which was first consumed, was good. None(9) of those who drank of it found fault with it; and the Lord partook of it also. But that wine was better which the Word made from water, on the moment, and simply for the use of those who had been called to the marriage. For although the Lord had the power to supply wine to those feasting, independently of any created substance, and to fill with food those who were hungry, He did not adopt this course; but, taking the loaves which the earth had produced, and giving thanks,(10) and on the other occasion making water wine, He satisfied those who were reclining [at table], and gave drink to those who had been invited to the marriage; showing that the God who made the earth, and commanded it to bring forth fruit, who established the waters, and brought forth the fountains, was He who in these last times bestowed upon mankind, by His Son, the blessing of food and the favour of drink: the Incomprehensible [acting thus] by means of the comprehensible, and the Invisible by the visible; since there is none beyond Him, but He exists in the bosom of the Father.

6. For "no man," he says, "hath seen God at any time," unless "the only–begotten Son of God, which is in the bosom of the Father, He hath declared [Him]."(11) For He, the Son who is in His bosom, declares to all the Father who is invisible. Wherefore they know Him to whom the Son reveals Him; and again, the Father, by means of the Son, gives knowledge of His Son to those who love Him. By whom also Nathanael, being taught, recognised [Him], he to whom also the Lord bare witness, that he was "an Israelite indeed, in whom was no guile."(12) The Israelite recognised his King, therefore did he cry out to Him, "Rabbi, Thou art the Son of God, Thou art the King of Israel." By whom also Peter, having been taught, recognised Christ as the Son of the living God, when [God] said, "Behold My dearly beloved Son, in whom I am well pleased: I will put my Spirit upon Him, and He shall show judgment to the Gentiles. He shall not strive, nor cry; neither shall any man hear His voice in the streets. A bruised reed shall He not break, and smoking flax shall He not quench, until He send forth judgment into contention ;(1) and in His name shall the Gentiles trust."(2)

7. Such, then, are the first principles of the Gospel: that there is one God, the Maker of this universe; He who was also announced by the prophets, and who by Moses set forth the dispensation of the law,—[principles] which proclaim the Father of our Lord Jesus Christ, and ignore any other God or Father except Him. So firm is the ground upon which these Gospels rest, that the very heretics themselves bear witness to them, and, starting from these [documents], each one of them endeavours to establish his own peculiar doctrine. For the Ebionites, who use Matthew's Gospel(3) only, are confuted out of this very same, making false suppositions with regard to the Lord. But Marcion, mutilating that according to Luke, is proved to be a blasphemer of the only existing God, from those [passages] which he still retains. Those, again, who separate Jesus from Christ, alleging that Christ remained impassible, but that it was Jesus who suffered, preferring the Gospel by Mark, if they read it with a love of truth, may have their errors rectified. Those, moreover, who follow Valentinus, making copious use of that according to John, to illustrate their conjunctions, shall be proved to be totally in error by means of this very Gospel, as I have shown in the first book. Since, then, our opponents do bear testimony to us, and make use of these [documents], our proof derived from them is firm and true.

8. It is not possible that the Gospels can be either more or fewer in number than they are. For, since there are four zones of the world in which we live, and four principal winds,(4) while the Church is scattered throughout all the world, and the "pillar and ground"(5) of the Church is the Gospel and the spirit of life; it is fitting that she should have four

pillars, breathing out immortality on every side, and vivifying men afresh. From which fact, it is evident that the Word, the Artificer of all, He that sitteth upon the cherubim, and contains all things, He who was manifested to men, has given us the Gospel under four aspects, but bound together by one Spirit. As also David says, when entreating His manifestation, "Thou that sittest between the cherubim, shine forth."(6) For the cherubim, too, were four-faced, and their faces were images of the dispensation of the Son of God. For, [as the Scripture] says, "The first living creature was like a lion,"(7) symbolizing His effectual working, His leadership, and royal power; the second [living creature] was like a calf, signifying [His] sacrificial and sacerdotal order; but "the third had, as it were, the face as of a man,"—an evident description of His advent as a human being; "the fourth was like a flying eagle," pointing out the gift of the Spirit hovering with His wings over the Church. And therefore the Gospels are in accord with these things, among which Christ Jesus is seated. For that according to John relates His original, effectual, and glorious generation from the Father, thus declaring, "In the beginning was the Word, and the Word was with God, and the Word was God."(8) Also, "all things were made by Him, and without Him was nothing made." For this reason, too, is that Gospel full of all confidence, for such is His person.(9) But that according to Luke, taking up [His] priestly character, commenced with Zacharias the priest offering sacrifice to God. For now was made ready the fatted calf, about to be immolated for(10) the finding again of the younger son. Matthew, again, relates His generation as a man, saying, "The book of the generation of Jesus Christ, the son of David, the son of Abraham;"(11) and also, "The birth of Jesus Christ was on this wise." This, then, is the Gospel of His humanity;(12) for which reason it is, too, that [the character of] a humble and meek man is kept up through the whole Gospel. Mark, on the other hand, commences with [a reference to] the prophetical spirit coming down from on high to men, saying, "The beginning of the Gospel of Jesus Christ, as it is written in Esaias the prophet,"—pointing to the winged aspect of the Gospel; and on this account he made a compendious and cursory narrative, for such is the prophetical character. And the Word of God Himself used to converse with the ante-Mosaic patriarchs, in accordance with His di- vinity and glory; but for those under the law he instituted a sacerdotal and liturgical service.(1) Afterwards, being made man for us, He sent the gift of the celestial Spirit over all the earth, protecting us with His wings. Such, then, as was the course followed by the Son of God, so was also the form of the living creatures; and such as was the form of the living creatures, so was also the character of the Gospel.(2) For the living creatures are quadriform, and the Gospel is quadriform, as is also the course followed by the Lord. For this reason were four principal (kaqolikai) covenants given to the human race:(3) one, prior to the deluge, under Adam; the second, that after the deluge, under Noah; the third, the giving of the law, under Moses; the fourth, that which renovates man, and sums up all things in itself by means of the Gospel, raising and bearing men upon heavenly kingdom.its wings into the

9. These things being so, all who destroy the form of the Gospel are vain, unlearned, and also audacious; those, [I mean,] who represent the aspects of the Gospel as being either more in number than as aforesaid, or, on the other hand, fewer. The former class [do so], that they may seem to have discovered more than is of the truth; the latter, that they may set the dispensations of God aside. For Marcion, rejecting the entire Gospel, yea rather, cutting himself off from the Gospel, boasts that he has part in the [blessings of] the Gospel.(4) Others, again (the Montanists), that they may set at nought the gift of the Spirit, which in the latter times has been, by the good pleasure of the Father, poured out upon the human race, do not admit that aspect [of the evangelical dispensation] presented by John's Gospel, in which the Lord promised that He would send the Paraclete;(5) but set aside at once both the Gospel and the prophetic Spirit. Wretched men indeed! who wish to be pseudo–prophets, forsooth, but who set aside the gift of prophecy

from the Church; acting like those (the Encratitae)(6) who, on account of such as come in hypocrisy, hold themselves aloof from the communion of the brethren. We must conclude, moreover, that these men (the Montanists) can not admit the Apostle Paul either. For, in his Epistle to the Corinthians,(7) he speaks expressly of prophetical gifts, and recognises men and women prophesying in the Church. Sinning, therefore, in all these particulars, against the Spirit of God,(8) they fall into the irremissible sin. But those who are from Valentinus, being, on the other hand, altogether reckless, while they put forth their own compositions, boast that they possess more Gospels than there really are. Indeed, they have arrived at such a pitch of audacity, as to entitle their comparatively recent writing "the Gospel of Truth," though it agrees in nothing with the Gospels of the Apostles, so that they have really no Gospel which is not full of blasphemy. For if what they have published is the Gospel of truth, and yet is totally unlike those which have been handed down to us from the apostles, any who please may learn, as is shown from the Scriptures themselves, that that which has been handed down from the apostles can no longer be reckoned the Gospel of truth. But that these Gospels alone are true and reliable, and admit neither an increase nor diminution of the aforesaid number, I have proved by so many and such [arguments]. For, since God made all things in due proportion and adaptation, it was fit also that the outward aspect of the Gospel should be well arranged and harmonized. The opinion of those men, therefore, who handed the Gospel down to us, having been investigated, from their very fountainheads, let us proceed also to the remaining apostles, and inquire into their doctrine with regard to God; then, in due course we shall listen to the very words of the Lord.

CHAP. XII. —DOCTRINE OF THE REST OF THE APOSTLES.

1. The Apostle Peter, therefore, after the resurrection of the Lord, and His assumption into the heavens, being desirous of filling up the number of the twelve apostles, and in electing into the place of Judas any substitute who should be chosen by God, thus addressed those who were present: "Men [and] brethren, this Scripture must needs have been fulfilled, which the Holy Ghost, by the mouth of David, spake before concerning Judas, which was made guide to them that took Jesus. For he was numbered with us:(9) ... Let his habitation be desolate, and let no man dwell therein;(1) and, His bishop–rick let another take;"(2)—thus leading to the completion of the apostles, according to the words spoken by David. Again, when the Holy Ghost had descended upon the disciples, that they all might prophesy and speak with tongues, and some mocked them, as if drunken with new wine, Peter said that they were not drunken, for it was the third hour of the day; but that this was what had been spoken by the prophet: "It shall come to pass in the last days, saith God, I will pour out of my Spirit upon all flesh, and they shall prophesy."(3) The God, therefore, who did promise by the prophet, that He would send His Spirit upon the whole human race, was He who did send; and God Himself is announced by Peter as having fulfilled His own promise.

2. For Peter said, "Ye men of Israel, hear my words; Jesus of Nazareth, a man approved by God among you by powers, and wonders, and signs, which God did by Him in the midst of you, as ye yourselves also know: Him, being delivered by the determined counsel and foreknowledge of God, by the hands of wicked men ye have slain, affixing [to the cross]: whom God hath raised up, having loosed the pains of death; because it was not possible that he should be holden of them. For David speaketh concerning Him,(4) I foresaw the Lord always before my face; for He is on my right hand, lest I should be moved: therefore did my heart rejoice, and my tongue was glad; moreover also, my flesh shall rest in hope: because Thou wilt not leave my soul in hell, neither wilt Thou give Thy Holy One to see corruption."(5) Then he proceeds to speak confidently to them concerning the patriarch David, that he was dead and buried, and that his sepulchre is

with them to this day. He said, "But since he was a prophet, and knew that God had sworn with an oath to him, that of the fruit of his body one should sit in his throne; foreseeing this, he spake of the resurrection of Christ, that He was not left in hell, neither did His flesh see corruption. This Jesus," he said, "hath God raised up, of which we all are witnesses: who, being exalted by the right hand of God, receiving from the Father the promise of the Holy Ghost, hath shed forth this gift(6) which ye now see and hear. For David has not ascended into the heavens; but he saith himself, The LORD said unto my Lord, Sit Thou on My fight hand, until I make Thy foes Thy footstool. Therefore let all the house of Israel know assuredly, that God hath made

[that same Jesus, whom ye have crucified, both Lord and Christ."(7) And when the multitudes exclaimed, "What shall we do then?" Peter says to them, "Repent, and be baptized every one of you in the name of Jesus for the remission of sins, and ye shall receive the gift of the Holy Ghost."(8) Thus the apostles did not preach another God, or another Fulness; nor, that the Christ who suffered and rose again was one, while he who flew off on high was another, and remained impossible; but that there was one and the same God the Father, and Christ Jesus who rose from the dead; and they preached faith in Him, to those who did not believe on the Son of God, and exhorted them out of the prophets, that the Christ whom God promised to send, He sent in Jesus, whom they crucified and God raised up.

3. Again, when Peter, accompanied by John, had looked upon the man lame from his birth, before that gate of the temple which is called Beautiful, sitting and seeking alms, he said to him, "Silver and gold I have none; but such as I have give I thee: In the name of Jesus Christ of Nazareth, rise up and walk. And immediately his legs and his feet received strength; and he walked, and entered with them into the temple, walking, and leaping, and praising God."(9) Then, when a multitude had gathered around them from all quarters because of this unexpected deed, Peter addressed them: "Ye men of Israel, why marvel ye at this; or why look ye so earnestly on us, as though by our own power we had made this man to walk? The God of Abraham, the God of Isaac, and the God of Jacob, the God of our fathers, hath glorified His Son, whom ye delivered up for judgment,(10) and denied in the presence of Pilate, when he wished to let Him go. But ye were bitterly set against(10) the Holy One and the Just, and desired a murderer to be granted unto you; but ye killed the Prince of life, whom God hath raised from the dead, whereof we are witnesses. And in the faith of His name, him, whom ye see and know, hath His name made strong; yea, the faith which is by Him, hath given him this perfect

soundness in the presence of you all. And now, brethren, I wot that through ignorance ye did this wickedness.(10) ... But those things which God before had showed by the mouth of all the prophets, that His Christ should suffer, He hath so fulfilled. Repent ye therefore, and be converted, that your sins may be blotted out, and that(11) the times of refresh– ing may come to you from the presence of the Lord; and He shall send Jesus Christ, prepared for you beforehand,(1) whom the heaven must indeed receive until the times of the arrangement(2) of all things, of which God hath spoken by His holy prophets. For Moses truly said unto our fathers, Your Lord God Shall raise up to you a Prophet from your brethren, like unto me; Him shall ye hear in all things whatsoever He shall say unto you. And it shall come to pass, that every soul, whosoever will not hear that Prophet, shall be destroyed from among the people. And all [the prophets] from Samuel, and henceforth, as many as have spoken, have likewise foretold of these days. Ye are the children of the prophets, and of the covenant which God made with our fathers, saying unto Abraham, And in thy seed shall all the kindreds of the earth be blessed. Unto you first, God, having raised up His Son, sent Him blessing you, that each may turn himself from his iniquities."(3) Peter, together with John, preached to them this plain message of glad tidings, that the promise which God made to the fathers had been fulfilled by Jesus; not certainly proclaiming another god, but the Son of God, who also was made man, and suffered; thus leading Israel into knowledge, and through Jesus preaching the resurrection of the dead,(4) and showing, that whatever the prophets had proclaimed as to the suffering of Christ, these had God fulfilled.

4. For this reason, too, when the chief priests were assembled, Peter, full of boldness, said to them, "Ye rulers of the people, and elders of Israel, if we this day be examined by you of the good deed done to the impotent man, by what means he has been made whole; be it known to you all, and to all the people of Israel, that by the name of Jesus Christ of Nazareth, whom ye crucified, whom God raised from the dead, even by Him cloth this man stand here before you whole. This is the stone which was set at nought of you builders, which is become the head–stone of the corner. [Neither is there salvation in any other: for] there is none other name under heaven, which is given to men, whereby we must be saved:"(5) Thus the apostles did not change God, but preached to the people that Christ was Jesus the crucified One, whom the same God that had sent the prophets, being God Himself, raised up, and gave in Him salvation to men.

5. They were confounded, therefore, both by this instance of healing ("for the man was above forty years old on whom this miracle of healing

took place"(6)), and by the doctrine of the apostles, and by the exposition of the prophets, when the chief priests had sent away Peter and John. [These latter] returned to the rest of their fellow–apostles and disciples of the Lord, that is, to the Church, and related what had occurred, and how courageously they had acted in the name of Jesus. The whole Church, it is then said, "when they had heard that, lifted up the voice to God with one accord, and said, Lord, Thou art God, which hast made heaven, and earth, and the sea, and all that in them is; who, through the Holy Ghost,(7) by the mouth of our father David, Thy servant, hast said, Why did the heathen rage, and the people imagine vain things? The kings of the earth stood up, and the rulers were gathered together against the Lord, and against His Christ. For of a truth, in this city,(8) against Thy holy Son Jesus, whom Thou hast anointed, both Herod and Pontius Pilate, with the Gentiles, and the people of Israel, were gathered together, to do whatsoever Thy hand and Thy counsel determined before to be done."(9) These [are the] voices of the Church from which every Church had its origin; these are the voices of the metropolis of the citizens of the new covenant; these are the voices of the apostles; these are voices of the disciples of the Lord, the truly perfect, who, after the assumption of the Lord, were perfected by the Spirit, and called upon the God who made heaven, and earth, and the sea,—who was announced by the prophets,—and Jesus Christ His Son, whom God anointed, and who knew no other [God]. For at that time and place there was neither Valentinus, nor Marcion, nor the rest of these subverters [of the truth], and their adherents. Wherefore God, the Maker of all things, heard them. For it is said, "The place was shaken where they were assembled together; and they were all filled with the Holy Ghost, and they spake the word of God with boldness"(10) to every one that was willing to believe.(11) "And with great power," it is added, "gave the apostles witness of the resurrection of the Lord Jesus,"(12) saying to them, "The God of our fathers raised up Jesus, whom ye seized and slew, hanging [Him] upon a beam of wood: Him hath God raised up by His right hand(13) to be a Prince and Saviour, to give repentance to Israel, and forgiveness of sins. And we are in this witnesses of these words; as also is the Holy Ghost, whom God hath given to them that believe in Him."(1) "And daily," it is said, "in the temple, and from house to house, they ceased not to teach and preach Christ Jesus,"(2) the Son of God. For this was the knowledge of salvation, which renders those who acknowledge His Son's advent perfect towards God.

6. But as some of these men impudently assert that the apostles, when preaching among the Jews, could not declare to them another god besides Him in whom they (their hearers(3)) believed, we say to them, that if the apostles used to speak to people in

accordance with the opinion instilled into them of old, no one learned the truth from them, nor, at a much earlier date, from the Lord; for they say that He did Himself speak after the same fashion. Wherefore neither do these men themselves know the truth; but since such was their opinion regarding God, they had just received doctrine as they were able to hear it. According to this manner of speaking, therefore, the rule of truth can be with nobody; but all learners will ascribe this practice to all [teachers], that just as every person thought, and as far as his capability extended, so was also the language addressed to him. But the advent of the Lord will appear superfluous and useless, if He did indeed come intending to tolerate and to preserve each man's idea regarding God rooted in him from of old. Besides this, also, it was a much heavier task, that He whom the Jews had seen as a man, and had fastened to the cross, should be preached as Christ the Son of God, their eternal King. Since this, however, was so, they certainly did not speak to them in accordance with their old belief. For they, who told them to their face that they were the slayers of the Lord, would themselves also much more boldly preach that Father who is above the Demiurge, and not what each individual bid himself believe [respecting God]; and the sin was much less, if indeed they had not fastened to the cross the superior Saviour (to whom it behoved them to ascend), since He was impassible. For, as they did not speak to the Gentiles in compliance with their notions, but told them with boldness that their gods were no gods, but the idols of demons; so would they in like manner have preached to the Jews, if they had known another greater or more perfect Father, not nourishing nor strengthening the untrue opinion of these men regarding God. Moreover, while destroying the error of the Gentiles, and bearing them away from their gods, they did not certainly induce another error upon them; but, removing

those which were no gods, they pointed out Him who alone was God and the true Father.

7. From the words of Peter, therefore, which he addressed in Caesarea to Cornelius the centurion, and those Gentiles with him, to whom the word of God was first preached, we can understand what the apostles used to preach, the nature of their preaching, and their idea with regard to God. For this Cornelius was, it is said, "a devout man, and one who feared God with all his house, giving much alms to the people, and praying to God always. He saw therefore, about the ninth hour of the day, an angel of God coming in to him, and saying, Thine alms are come up for a memorial before God. Wherefore send to Simon, who is called Peter."(4) But when Peter saw the vision, in which the voice from heaven said to him, "What God hath cleansed, that call not thou common,"(5) this happened [to teach him] that the God who had, through the law, distinguished between

clean and unclean, was He who had purified the Gentiles through the blood of His Son—He whom also Cornelius worshipped; to whom Peter, coming in, said, "Of a truth I perceive that God is no respecter of persons: but in every nation, he that feareth Him, and worketh righteousness, is acceptable to Him."(6) He thus clearly indicates, that He whom Cornelius had previously feared as God, of whom he had heard through the law and the prophets, for whose sake also he used to give alms, is, in truth, God. the knowledge of the Son was, however, wanting to him; therefore did [Peter] add, "The word, ye know, which was published throughout all Judea, beginning from Galilee, after the baptism which John preached, Jesus of Nazareth, how God anointed Him with the Holy Ghost, and with power; who went about doing good, and healing all that were oppressed of the devil; for God was with Him. And we are witnesses of all those things which He did both in the land of the Jews and in Jerusalem; whom they slew, hanging Him on a beam of wood: Him God raised up the third day, and showed Him openly; not to all the people, but unto us, witnesses chosen before of God, who did eat and drink with Him after the resurrection from the dead. And He commanded us to preach unto the people, and to testify that it is He which was ordained of God to be the Judge of quick and dead. To Him give all the prophets witness, that, through His name, every one that believeth in Him does receive remission of sins."(7) The apostles, therefore, did preach the Son of God, of whom men were ignorant; and His advent, to those who had been already instructed as to God; but they did not bring in another god. For if Peter had known any such thing, he would have preached freely to the Gentiles, that the God of the Jews was indeed one, but the God of the Christians another; and all of them, doubtless, being awe-struck because of the vision of the angel, would have believed whatever he told them. But it is evident from Peter's words that he did indeed still retain the God who was already known to them; but he also bare witness to them that Jesus Christ was the Son of God, the Judge of quick and dead, into whom he did also command them to be baptized for the remission of sins; and not this alone, but he witnessed that Jesus was Himself the Son of God, who also, having been anointed with the Holy Spirit, is called Jesus Christ. And He is the same being that was born of Mary, as the testimony of Peter implies. Can it really be, that Peter was not at that time as yet in possession of the perfect knowledge which these men discovered afterwards? According to them, therefore, Peter was imperfect, and the rest of the apostles were imperfect; and so it would be fitting that they, coming to life again, should become disciples of these men, in order that they too might be made perfect. But this is truly ridiculous. These men, in fact, are proved to be not disciples of the apostles, but of their own wicked notions. To this cause also are due the various opinions which exist among them, inasmuch as each one adopted error just as he was capable(1) [of embracing it]. But the Church throughout all the world, having its origin finn from the apostles, perseveres in one and the same opinion with regard to God and His Son.

8. But again: Whom did Philip preach to the eunuch of the queen of the Ethiopians, returning from Jerusalem, and reading Esaias the prophet, when he and this man were alone together? Was it not He of whom the prophet spoke: "He was led as a sheep to the slaughter, and as a lamb dumb before the shearer, so He opened not the month?" "But who shall declare His nativity? for His life shall be taken away from the earth."(2) [Philip declared] that this was Jesus, and that the Scripture was fulfilled in Him; as did also the believing eunuch himself: and, immediately requesting to be baptized, he said, "I believe Jesus Christ to be the Son of God."(3) This man was also sent into the regions of Ethiopia, to preach what he had himself believed, that there was one God preached by the prophets, but that the Son of this [God] had

already made [His] appearance in human nature (secundum hominem), and had been led as a sheep to the slaughter; and all the other statements which the prophets made regarding Him.

9. Paul himself also—after that the Lord spoke to him out of heaven, and showed him that, in persecuting His disciples, he persecuted his own Lord, and sent Ananias to him that he might recover his sight, and be baptized–"preached," it is said, "Jesus in the synagogues at Damascus, with all freedom of speech, that this is the Son of God, the Christ."(4) This is the mystery which he says was made known to him by revelation, that He who suffered under Pontius Pilate, the same is Lord of all, and King, and God, and Judge, receiving power from Him who is the God of all, because He became "obedient unto death, even the death of the cross."(5) And inasmuch as this is true, when [preaching to the Athenians on the Areopagus—where, no Jews being present, he had it in his power to preach God with freedom of speech—he said to them: "God, who made the world, and all things therein, He, being Lord of heaven and earth, dwelleth not in temples made with hands; neither is He touched(6) by men's hands, as though He needed anything, seeing He giveth to all life, and breath, and all things; who hath made from one blood the whole race of men to dwell upon the face of the whole earth,(7) predetermining the times according to the boundary of their habitation, to seek the Deity, if by any means they might be able to track Him out, or find Him, although He be not far from each of us. For in Him we live, and move, and have our being, as certain men of your own have said, For we are also His offspring. Inasmuch, then, as we are the offspring of God, we ought not

to think that the Deity is like unto gold or silver, or stone graven by art or man's device. Therefore God, winking at the times of ignorance, does now command all men everywhere to turn to Him with repentance; because He hath appointed a day, on which the world shall be judged in righteousness by the man Jesus; whereof He hath given assurance by raising, Him from the dead."(8) Now in this passage he does not only declare to them God as the Creator of the world, no Jews being present, but that He did also make one race of men to dwell upon all the earth; as also Moses declared: "When the Most High divided the nations, as He scattered the sons of Adam, He set the bounds of the nations after the number of the angels of God;"(9) but that people which believes in God is not now under the power of angels, but under the Lord's [rule]. "For His people Jacob was made the portion of the Lord, Israel the cord of His inheritance."(1) And again, at Lystra of Lycia (Lycaonia), when Paul was with Barnabas, and in the name of our Lord Jesus Christ had made a man to walk who had been lame from his birth, and when the crowd wished to honour them as gods because of the astonishing deed, he said to them: "We are men like unto you, preaching to you God, that ye may be turned away from these vain idols to [serve] the living God, who made heaven, and earth, and the sea, and all things that are therein; who in times past suffered all nations to walk in their own ways, although He left not Himself without witness, performing acts of goodness, giving you rain from heaven, and fruitful seasons, filling your hearts with food and gladness."(2) But that all his Epistles are consonant to these declarations, I shall, when expounding the apostle, show from the Epistles themselves, in the right place. But while I bring out by these proofs the truths of Scripture, and set forth briefly and compendiously things which are stated in various ways, do thou also attend to them with patience, and not deem them prolix; taking this into account, that proofs [of the things which are] contained in the Scriptures cannot be shown except from the Scriptures themselves.

10. And still further, Stephen, who was chosen the first deacon by the apostles, and who, of all men, was the first to follow the footsteps of the martyrdom of the Lord, being the first that was slain for confessing Christ, speaking boldly among the people, and teaching them, says: "The God of glory appeared to our father Abraham, ... and said to him, Get thee out of thy country, and from thy kindred, and come into the land which I shall show thee; ... and He removed him into this land, wherein ye now dwell. And He gave him none inheritance in it, no, not so much as to set his foot on; yet He promised that He would give it to him for a possession, and to his seed after him. ... And God spake on this wise, That his seed should sojourn in a strange land, and should be brought into bondage, and should be evil−entreated four hundred years; and the nation whom they shall serve

will I judge, says the Lord. And after that shall they come forth, and serve me in this place. And He gave him the covenant of circumcision: and so [Abraham] begat Isaac."(3) And the rest of his words announce the same God, who was with Joseph and with the patriarchs, and who spake with Moses.

11. And that the whole range of the doctrine of the apostles proclaimed one and the same God, who removed Abraham, who made to him the promise of inheritance, who in due season gave to him the covenant of circumcision, who called his descendants out of Egypt, preserved outwardly by circumcision—for he gave it as a sign, that they might not be like the Egyptians—that He was the Maker of all things, that He was the Father of our Lord Jesus Christ, that He was the God of glory,—they who wish may learn from the very words and acts of the apostles, and may contemplate the fact that this God is one, above whom is no other. But even if there were another god above Him, we should say, upon [instituting] a comparison of the quantity [of the work done by each], that the latter is superior to the former. For by deeds the better man appears, as I have already remarked;(4) and, inasmuch as these men have no works of their father to adduce, the latter is shown to be God alone. But if any one, "doting about questions,"(5) do imagine that what the apostles have declared about God should be allegorized, let him consider my previous statements, in which I set forth one God as the Founder and Maker of all things, and destroyed and laid bare their allegations; and he shah find them agreeable to the doctrine of the apostles, and so to maintain what they used to teach, and were persuaded of, that there is one God, the Maker of all things. And when he shall have divested his mind of such error, and of that blasphemy against God which it implies, he will of himself find reason to acknowledge that both the Mosaic law and the grace of the new covenant, as both fitted for the times [at which they were given], were bestowed by one and the same God for the benefit of the human race.

12. For all those who are of a perverse mind, having been set against the Mosaic legislation, judging it to be dissimilar and contrary to the doctrine of the Gospel, have not applied themselves to investigate the causes of the difference of cach covenant. Since, therefore, they have been deserted by the paternal love, and puffed up by Satan, being brought over to the doctrine of Simon Magus, they have apostatized in their opinions from Him who is God, and imagined that they have themselves discovered more than the apostles, by finding out another god; and [maintained] that the apostles preached the Gospel still somewhat under the influence of Jewish opinions, but that they themselves are purer [in doctrine], and more intelligent, than the apostles. Wherefore also Marcion

and his followers have betaken themselves to mutilating the Scriptures, not acknowledging some books at all; and, curtailing the Gospel according to Luke and the Epistles of Paul, they assert that these are alone authentic, which they have themselves thus shortened. In another work,(1) however, I shall, God granting [me strength], refute them out of these which they still retain. But all the rest, inflated with the false name of "knowledge," do certainly recognise the Scriptures; but they pervert the interpretations, as I have shown in the first book. And, indeed, the followers of Marcion do directly blaspheme the Creator, alleging him to be the creator of evils, [but] holding a more tolerable(2) theory as to his origin, [and] maintaining that there are two beings, gods by nature, differing from each other,—the one being good, but the other evil. Those from Valentinus, however, while they employ names of a more honourable kind, and set forth that He who is Creator is both Father, and Lord, and God, do [nevertheless] render their theory or sect more plasphemous, by maintaining that He was not produced from any one of those Aeons within the Pleroma, but from that defect which had been expelled beyond the Pleroma. Ignorance of the Scriptures and of the dispensation of God has brought all these things upon them. And in the course of this work I shall touch upon the cause of the difference of the covenants on the one hand, and, on the other hand, of their unity and harmony.

13. But that both the apostles and their disciples thus taught as the Church preaches, and thus teaching were perfected, wherefore also they were called away to that which is perfect—Stephen, teaching these truths, when he was yet on earth, saw the glory of God, and Jesus on His right hand, and exclaimed, "Behold, I see the heavens opened, and the Son of man standing on the right hand of God."(3) These words he said, and was stoned; and thus did he fulfil the perfect doctrine, copying in every respect the Leader of martyrdom, and praying for those who were slaying him, in these words: "Lord, lay not this sin to their charge." Thus were they perfected who knew one and the same God, who from beginning to end was present with mankind in the various dispensations; as the prophet Hosea declares: "I have filled up visions, and used similitudes by the hands of the prophets."(4) Those, therefore, who delivered up their souls to death for Christ's Gospel—how could they have spoken to men in accordance with old-established opinion? If this had been the course adopted by them, they should not have suffered; but inasmuch as they did preach

things contrary to those persons who did not assent to the truth, for that reason they suffered. It is evident, therefore, that they did not relinquish the truth, but with all boldness preached to the Jews and Greeks. To the Jews, indeed, [they proclaimed] that the Jesus who was crucified by them was the Son of God, the Judge of quick and dead, and that He has received from His Father an eternal kingdom in Israel, as I have pointed out; but to the Greeks they preached one God, who made all things, and Jesus Christ His Son.

14. This is shown in a still clearer light from the letter of the apostles, which they forwarded neither to the Jews nor to the Greeks, but to those who from the Gentiles believed in Christ, confirming their faith. For when certain men had come down from Judea to Antioch—where also, first of all, the Lord's disciples were called Christians, because of their faith in Christ—and sought to persuade those who had believed on the Lord to be circumcised, and to perform other things after the observance of the law; and when Paul and Barnabas had gone up to Jerusalem to the apostles on account of this question, and the whole Church had convened together, Peter thus addressed them: "Men, brethren, ye know how that from the days of old God made choice among you, that the Gentiles by my mouth should hear the word of the Gospel, and believe. And God, the Searcher of the heart, bare them witness, giving them the Holy Ghost, even as to us; and put no difference between us and them, purifying their hearts by faith. Now therefore why tempt ye God, to impose a yoke upon the neck of the disciples, which neither our fathers nor we were able to bear? But we believe that, through the grace of our Lord Jesus Christ, we are to be saved, even as they."(5) After him James spoke as follows: "Men, brethren, Simon hath declared how God did purpose to take from among the Gentiles a people for His name. And thus(6) do the words of the prophets agree, as it is written, After this I will return, and will build again the tabernacle of David, which is fallen down; and I will build the ruins thereof, and I will set it up: that the residue of men may seek after the Lord, and all the Gentiles, among whom my name has been invoked, saith the Lord, doing these things.(7) Known from eternity is His work to God. Wherefore I for my part give judgment, that we trouble not them who from among the Gentiles are turned to God: but that it be enjoined them, that they do abstain from the vanities of idols, and from fornication, and from blood; and whatsoever(1) they wish not to be done to themselves, let them not do to others."(2) And when these things had been said, and all had given their consent, they wrote to them after this manner: "The apostles, and the presbyters, [and] the brethren, unto those brethren from among the Gentiles who are in Antioch, and Syria, and Cilicia, greeting: Forasmuch as we have heard that certain persons going out from us have troubled you with words, subverting your souls, saying, Ye must be circumcised, and keep the law; to whom we gave no such commandment: it

seemed good unto us, being assembled with one accord, to send chosen men unto you with our beloved Barnabas and Paul; men who have delivered up their soul for the name of our Lord Jesus Christ. We have sent therefore Judas and Silas, that they may declare our opinion by word of mouth. For it seemed good to the Holy Ghost, and to us, to lay upon you no greater burden than these necessary things; that ye abstain from meats offered to idols, and from blood, and from fornication; and whatsoever ye do not wish to be done to you, do not ye to others: from which preserving yourselves, ye shall do well, walking(3) in the Holy Spirit." From all these passages, then, it is evident that they did not teach the existence of another Father, but gave the new covenant of liberty to those who had lately believed in God by the Holy Spirit. But they clearly indicated, from the nature of the point debated by them, as to whether or not it were still necessary to circumcise the disciples, that they had no idea of another god.

15. Neither [in that case] would they have had such a tenor with regard to the first covenant, as not even to have been willing to eat with the Gentiles. For even Peter, although he had been sent to instruct them, and had been constrained by a vision to that effect, spake nevertheless with not a little hesitation, saying to them: "Ye know how it is an unlawful thing for a man that is a Jew to keep company with, or to come unto, one of another nation; but God hath shown me that I should not call any man common or unclean. Therefore came I without gainsaying;"(4) indicating by these words, that he would not have come to them unless he had been commanded. Neither, for a like reason, would he have given them baptism so readily, had he not heard them prophesying when the Holy Ghost rested upon them. And therefore did he exclaim, "Can any man forbid water, that these

should not be baptized, who have received the Holy Ghost as well as we?"(5) He persuaded, at the same time, those that were with him, and pointed out that, unless the Holy Ghost had rested upon them, there might have been some one who would have raised objections to their baptism. And the apostles who were with James allowed the Gentiles to act freely, yielding us up to the Spirit of God. But they themselves, while knowing the same God, continued in the ancient observances; so that even Peter, fearing also lest he might incur their reproof, although formerly eating with the Gentiles, because of the vision, and of the Spirit who had rested upon them, yet, when certain persons came from James, withdrew himself, and did not eat with them. And Paul said that Barnabas likewise did the same thing.(6) Thus did the apostles, whom the Lord made witnesses of every action and of every doctrine—for upon all occasions do we find Peter, and James, and John present with Him—scrupulously act according to the dispensation of the Mosaic law, showing that it was from one and the same God; which they certainly never would have done, as I have already said, if they had learned from the Lord [that there existed] another Father besides Him who appointed the dispensation of the law.

CHAP. XIII—REFUTATION OF THE OPINION, THAT PAUL WAS THE ONLY APOSTLE WHO HAD KNOWLEDGE OF THE TRUTH.

1. With regard to those (the Marcionites) who allege that Paul alone knew the truth, and that to him the mystery was manifested by revelation, let Paul himself convict them, when he says, that one and the same God wrought in Peter for the apostolate of the circumcision, and in himself for the Gentiles.(7) Peter, therefore, was an apostle of that very God whose was also Paul; and Him whom Peter preached as God among those of the circumcision, and likewise the Son of God, did Paul [declare] also among the Gentiles. For our Lord never came to save Paul alone, nor is God so limited in means, that He should have but one apostle who knew the dispensation of His Son. And again, when Paul says, "How beautiful are the feet of those bringing glad tidings of good things, and preaching the Gospel of peace,"(8) he shows clearly that it was not merely one, but there were many who used to preach the truth. And again, in the Epistle to the Corinthians, when he had recounted all those who had seen God(9) after the resurrection, he says in continuation, "But whether it were I or they, so we preach, and so ye believed, "(1) acknowledging as one and the same, the preaching of all those who saw God(2) after the resurrection from the dead.

2. And again, the Lord replied to Philip, who wished to behold the Father, "Have I been so long a time with you, and yet thou hast not known Me, Philip? He that sees Me, sees also the Father; and how sayest thou then, Show us the Father? For I am in the Father, and the Father in Me; and henceforth ye know Him, and have seen Him." (3) To these men, therefore, did the Lord bear witness, that in Himself they had both known and seen the Father (and the Father is truth). To allege, then, that these men did not know the truth, is to act the part of false witnesses, and of those who have been alienated from the doctrine of Christ. For why did the Lord send the twelve apostles to the lost sheep of the house of Israel,(4) if these men did not know the truth? How also did the seventy preach, unless they had themselves previously known the truth of what was preached? Or how

could Peter have been in ignorance, to whom the Lord gave testimony, that flesh and blood had not revealed to him, but the Father, who is in heaven?(5) Just, then, as" Paul [was] an apostle, not of men, neither by man, but by Jesus Christ, and God the Father,"(6) [so with the rest;] (7) the Son indeed leading them to the Father, but the Father revealing to them the Son.

3. But that Paul acceded to [the request of] those who summoned him to the apostles, on account of the question [which had been raised], and went up to them, with Barnabas, to Jerusalem, not without reason, but that the liberty of the Gentiles might be confirmed by them, he does himself say, in the Epistle to the Galatians: "Then, fourteen years after, I went up again to Jerusalem with Barnabas, taking also Titus. But I went up by revelation, and communicated to them that Gospel which I preached among the Gentiles."(8) And again he says, "For an hour we did give place to subjection,(9) that the truth of the gospel might continue with you." If, then, any one shall, from the Acts of the Apostles, carefully scrutinize the time concerning which it is written that he went up to Jerusalem on account of the forementioned question, he will find those years mentioned by Paul coinciding with it. Thus the statement of Paul harmonizes with, and is, as it were, identical with, the testimony of Luke regarding the apostles.

CHAP. XIV.—IF PAUL HAD KNOWN ANY MYSTERIES UNREVEALED TO THE OTHER APOSTLES, LUKE, HIS CONSTANT COMPANION AND FELLOW–TRAVELLER, COULD NOT HAVE BEEN IGNORANT OF THEM; NEITHER COULD THE TRUTH HAVE POSSIBLY LAIN HID FROM HIM, THROUGH WHOM ALONE WE LEARN MANY AND MOST IMPORTANT PARTICULARS OF THE GOSPEL HISTORY.

1. But that this Luke was inseparable from Paul, and his fellow–labourer in the Gospel, he himself clearly evinces, not as a matter of boasting, but as bound to do so by the truth itself. For he says that when Barnabas, and John who was called Mark, had parted company from Paul, and sailed to Cyprus, "we came to Troas;"(10) and when Paul had beheld in a dream a man of Macedonia, saying, "Come into Macedonia, Paul, and help us," "immediately," he says, "we endeavoured to go into Macedonia, understanding that the Lord had called us to preach the Gospel unto them. Therefore, sailing from Troas, we

directed our ship's course towards Samothracia." And then he carefully indicates all the rest of their journey as far as Philippi, and how they delivered their first address: "for, sitting down," he says, "we spake unto the women who had assembled;"(11) and certain believed, even a great many. And again does he say, "But we sailed from Philippi after the days of unleavened bread, and came to Troas, where we abode seven days."(12) And all the remaining [details] of his course with Paul he recounts, indicating with all diligence both places, and cities, and number of days, until they went up to Jerusalem; and what befell Paul there,(13) how he was sent to Rome in bonds; the name of the centurion who took him in charge;(14) and the signs of the ships, and how they made shipwreck;(15) and the island upon which they escaped, and how they received kindness there, Paul healing the chief man of that island; and how they sailed from thence to Puteoli, and from that arrived at Rome; and for what period they sojourned at Rome. As Luke was present at all these occurrences, he carefully noted them down in writing, so that he cannot be convicted of falsehood or boastfulness, because all these [particulars] proved both that he was senior to all those who now teach otherwise, and that he was not ignorant of the truth. That he was not merely a follower, but also a fellow–labourer of the apostles, but especially of Paul, Paul has himself declared also in the Epistles, saying: "Demas hath forsaken me, ... and is departed unto Thessalonica; Crescens to Galatia, Titus to Dalmatia. Only Luke is with me."(1) From this he shows that he was always attached to and inseparable from him. And again he says, in the Epistle to the Colossians: "Luke, the beloved physician, greets you."(2) But surely if Luke, who always preached in company with Paul, and is called by him "the beloved," and with him performed the work of an evangelist, and was entrusted to hand down to us a Gospel, learned nothing different from him (Paul), as has been pointed out from his words, how can these men, who were never attached to Paul, boast that they have learned hidden and unspeakable mysteries?

2. But that Paul taught with simplicity what he knew, not only to those who were [employed] with him, but to those that heard him, he does himself make manifest. For when the bishops and presbyters who came from Ephesus and the other cities adjoining had assembled in Miletus, since he was himself hastening to Jerusalem to observe Pentecost, after testifying many things to them, and declaring what must happen to him at Jerusalem, he added: "I know that ye shall see my face no more. Therefore I take you to record this day, that I am pure from the blood of all. For I have not shunned to declare unto you all the counsel of God. Take heed, therefore, both to yourselves, and to all the flock over which the Holy Ghost has placed you as bishops, to rule the Church of the

Lord,(3) which He has acquired for Himself through His own blood."(4) Then, referring to the evil teachers who should arise, he said: "I know that after my departure shall grievous wolves come to you, not sparing the flock. Also of your own selves shall men arise, speaking perverse things, to draw away disciples after them." "I have not shunned," he says, "to declare unto you all the counsel of God." Thus did the apostles simply, and without respect of persons, deliver to all what they had themselves learned from the Lord. Thus also does Luke, without respect of persons, deliver to us what he had learned from them, as he has himself testified, saying, "Even as they delivered them unto us, who from the beginning were eye–witnesses and ministers of the Word."(5)

3. Now if any man set Luke aside, as one who did not know the truth, he will, [by so acting,]

manifestly reject that Gospel of which he claims to be a disciple. For through him we have become acquainted with very many and important parts of the Gospel; for instance, the generation of John, the history of Zacharias, the coming of the angel to Mary, the exclamation of Elisabeth, the descent of the angels to the shepherds, the words spoken by them, the testimony of Anna and of Simeon with regard to Christ, and that twelve years of age He was left behind at Jerusalem; also the baptism of John, the number of the Lord's years when He was baptized, and that this occurred in the fifteenth year of Tiberius Caesar. And in His office of teacher this is what He has said to the rich: "Woe unto you that are rich, for ye have received your consolation;"(6) and "Woe unto you that are full, for ye shall hunger; and ye who laugh now, for ye shall weep;" and, "Woe unto you when all men shall speak well of you: for so did your fathers to the false prophets." All things of the following kind we have known through Luke alone (and numerous actions of the Lord we have learned through him, which also all [the Evangelists] notice): the multitude of fishes which Peter's companions enclosed, when at the Lord's command they cast the nets;(7) the woman who had suffered for eighteen years, and was healed on the Sabbath–day;(8) the man who had the dropsy, whom the Lord made whole on the Sabbath, and how He did defend Himself for having performed an act of healing on that day; how He taught His disciples not to aspire to the uppermost rooms; how we should invite the poor and feeble, who cannot recompense us; the man who knocked during the night to obtain loaves, and did obtain them, because of the urgency of his importunity;(9) how, when [our Lord] was sitting at meat with a Pharisee, a woman that was a sinner kissed His feet, and anointed them with ointment, with what the Lord said to Simon on her behalf concerning the two debtors;(10) also about the parable of that rich man who stored up the goods which had accrued to him, to whom it was also said, "In this night they shall demand thy soul from thee; whose then shall those things be which thou hast prepared?"(11) and similar to this, that of the rich man, who was clothed in purple and who fared sumptuously, and the indigent Lazarus;(12) also the answer which He gave to His disciples when they said, "Increase our faith;"(13) also His conversation with Zaccheus the publican;(14) also about the Pharisee and the publican, who were praying in the temple at the same time;(1) also the ten lepers, whom He cleansed in the way simultaneously;(2) also how He ordered the lame and the blind to be gathered to the wedding from the lanes and streets;(3) also the parable of the judge who feared not God, whom the widow's importunity led to avenge her cause;(4) and about the fig-tree in the vineyard which produced no fruit. There are also many other particulars to be found mentioned by Luke alone, which are made use of by both Marcion and Valentinus. And besides all these, [he records] what [Christ] said to His disciples in the way, after the resurrection, and how they recognised Him in the breaking of bread.(5)

4. It follows then, as of course, that these men must either receive the rest of his narrative, or else reject these parts also. For no persons of common sense can permit them to receive some things recounted by Luke as being true, and to set others aside, as if he had not known the truth. And if indeed Marcion's followers reject these, they will then possess no Gospel; for, curtailing that according to Luke, as I have said already, they boast in having the Gospel [in what remains]. But the followers of Valentinus must give up their utterly vain talk; for they have taken from that [Gospel] many occasions for their own speculations, to put an evil interpretation upon what he has well said. If, on the other hand, they feel compelled to receive the remaining portions also, then, by studying the perfect Gospel, and the doctrine of the apostles, they will find it necessary to repent, that they may be saved from the danger [to which they are exposed].

CHAP. XV.—REFUTATION OF THE EBIONITES, WHO DISPARAGED THE AUTHORITY OF ST. PAUL, FROM THE WRITINGS OF ST. LUKE, WHICH MUST BE RECEIVED AS A WHOLE. EXPOSURE OF THE HYPOCRISY, DECEIT, AND PRIDE OF THE GNOSTICS. THE APOSTLES AND THEIR DISCIPLES KNEW AND PREACHED ONE GOD, THE CREATOR OF THE WORLD.

1. But again, we allege the same against those who do not recognise Paul as an apostle: that they should either reject the other words of the Gospel which we have come to know through Luke alone, and not make use of them; or else, if they do receive all these, they must necessarily admit also that testimony concerning Paul, when he (Luke) tells us that the Lord spoke at first to him from heaven: "Saul, Saul, why persecutest thou Me? I am Jesus Christ, whom thou persecutest; "(6) and then to Ananias, saying regarding him: "Go thy way; for he is a chosen vessel unto Me, to bear My name among the Gentiles, and kings, and the children of Israel. For I will show him, from this time, how great things he must suffer for My name's sake."(7) Those, therefore, who do not accept of him [as a teacher], who was chosen by God for this purpose, that he might boldly bear His name, as being sent to the forementioned nations, do despise the election of God, and separate themselves from the company of the apostles. For neither can they contend that Paul was no apostle, when he was chosen for this purpose; nor can they prove Luke guilty of falsehood, when he proclaims the truth to us with all diligence. It may be, indeed, that it was with this view that God set forth very many Gospel truths, through Luke's instrumentality, which all should esteem it necessary to use, in order that all persons, following his subsequent testimony, which treats upon the acts and the doctrine of the apostles, and holding the unadulterated rule of truth, may be saved. His testimony, therefore, is true, and the doctrine of the apostles is open and stedfast, holding nothing in reserve; nor did they teach one set of doctrines in private, and another in public.

2. For this is the subterfuge of false persons, evil seducers, and hypocrites, as they act who are from Valentinus. These men discourse to the multitude about those who belong to the Church, whom they do themselves term "vulgar," and "ecclesiastic."(8) By these words they entrap the more simple, and entice them, imitating our phraseology, that these [dupes] may listen to them the oftener; and then these are asked(9) regarding us, how it is, that when they hold doctrines similar to ours, we, without cause, keep ourselves aloof from their company; and [how it is, that] when they say the same things, and hold the same doctrine, we call them heretics? When they have thus, by means of questions, overthrown the faith of any, and rendered them uncontradicting hearers of their own, they describe to them in private the unspeakable mystery of their Pleroma. But they are altogether deceived, who imagine that they may learn from the Scriptural texts adduced by heretics, that [doctrine] which their words plausibly teach.(10) For error is plausible, and bears a re– semblance to the truth, but requires to be disguised; while truth is without disguise, and therefore has been entrusted to children. And if any one of their auditors do indeed demand explanations, or start objections to them, they affirm that he is one not

capable of receiving the truth, and not having from above the seed [derived] from their Mother; and thus really give him no reply, but simply declare that he is of the intermediate regions, that is, belongs to animal natures. But if any one do yield himself up to them like a little sheep, and follows out their practice, and their "redemption," such an one is puffed up to such an extent, that he thinks he is neither in heaven nor on earth, but that he has passed within the Pleroma; and having already embraced his angel, he walks with a strutting gait and a supercilious countenance, possessing all the pompous air of a cock. There are those among them who assert that that man who comes from above ought to follow a good course of conduct; wherefore they do also pretend a gravity [of demeanour] with a certain superciliousness. The majority, however, having become scoffers also, as if already perfect, and living without regard [to appearances], yea, in contempt [of that which is good], call themselves "the spiritual," and allege that they have already become acquainted with that place of refreshing which is within their Pleroma.

3. But let us revert to the same line of argument [hitherto pursued]. For when it has been manifestly declared, that they who were the preachers of the truth and the apostles of liberty termed no one else God, or named him Lord, except the only true God the Father, and His Word, who has the pre–eminence in all things; it shall then be clearly proved, that they (the apostles) confessed as the Lord God Him who was the Creator of heaven and earth, who also spoke with Moses, gave to him the dispensation of the law, and who called the fathers; and that they knew no other. The opinion of the apostles, therefore, and of those (Marks and Luke) who learned from their words, concerning God, has been made manifest.

CHAP. XVI.—PROOFS FROM THE APOSTOLIC WRITINGS, THAT JESUS CHRIST WAS ONE AND THE SAME, THE ONLY BEGOTTEN SON OF GOD, PERFECT GOD AND PERFECT MAN.

1. But(1) there are some who say that Jesus was merely a receptacle of Christ, upon whom the Christ, as a dove, descended from above, and that when He had declared the unnameable Father He entered into the Pleroma in an incomprehensible and invisible manner: for that He was not comprehended, not only by men, but not even by those powers and virtues which are in heaven, and that Jesus was the Son, but that(2) Christ was the Father, and the Father of Christ, God; while others say that He merely suffered in

outward appearance, being naturally impassible. The Valentinians, again, maintain that the dispensational Jesus was the same who passed through Mary, upon whom that Saviour from the more exalted [region] descended, who was also termed Pan,(3) because He possessed the names (vocabula) of all those who had produced Him; but that [this latter] shared with Him, the dispensational one, His power and His name; so that by His means death was abolished, but the Father was made known by that Saviour who had descended from above, whom they do also allege to be Himself the receptacle of Christ and of the entire Pleroma; confessing, indeed, in tongue one Christ Jesus, but being divided in [actual] opinion: for, as I have already observed, it is the practice of these men to say that there was one Christ, who was produced by Monogenes, for the confirmation of the Pleroma; but that another, the Saviour, was sent [forth] for the glorification of the Father; and yet another, the dispensational one, and whom they represent as having suffered, who also bore [in himself] Christ, that Saviour who returned into the Pleroma. I judge it necessary therefore to take into account the entire mind of the apostles regarding our Lord Jesus Christ, and to show that not only did they never hold any such opinions regarding Him; but, still further, that they announced through the Holy Spirit, that those who should teach such doctrines were agents of Satan, sent forth for the purpose of overturning the faith of some, and drawing them away from life.

2. That John knew the one and the same Word of God, and that He was the only begotten, and that He became incarnate for our salvation, Jesus Christ our Lord, I have sufficiently proved from the word of John himself. And Matthew, too, recognising one and the same Jesus Christ, exhibiting his generation as a man from the Virgin,(4) even as God did promise David that He would raise up from the fruit of his body an eternal King, having made the same promise to Abraham a long time previously, says: "The book of the generation of Jesus Christ, the son of David, the son of Abraham"(5) Then, that he might free our mind from suspicion regarding Joseph, he says: "But the birth of Christ(6) was on this wise. When His mother was espoused to Joseph, before they came together, she was found with child of the Holy Ghost." Then, when Joseph had it in contemplation to put Mary away, since she proved with child, [Matthew tells us of] the angel of God standing by him, and saying: "Fear not to take unto thee Mary thy wife: for that which is conceived in her is of the Holy Ghost. And she shall bring forth a son, and thou shalt call His name Jesus; for He shall save His people from their sins. Now this was done, that it might be fulfilled which was spoken of the Lord by the prophet: Behold. a virgin shall conceive, and bring forth a son, and they shall call His name Emmanuel, which is, God with us;" clearly signifying that both the promise made to the fathers had been

accomplished, that the Son of God was born of a virgin, and that He Himself was Christ the Saviour whom the prophets had foretold; not, as these men assert, that Jesus was He who was born of Mary, but that Christ was He who descended from above. Matthew might certainly have said, "Now the birth of Jesus was on this wise;" but the Holy Ghost, foreseeing the corrupters [of the truth], and guarding by anticipation against their deceit, says by Matthew, "But the birth of Christ was on this wise;" and that He is Emmanuel, lest perchance we might consider Him as a mere man: for "not by the will of the flesh nor by the will of man, but by the will of God was the Word made flesh;"(1) and that we should not imagine that Jesus was one, and Christ another, but should know them to be one and the same.

3. Paul, when writing to the Romans, has explained this very point: "Paul, an apostle of Jesus Christ, predestinated unto the Gospel of God, which He had promised by His prophets in the holy Scriptures, concerning His Son, who was made to Him of the seed of David according to the flesh, who was predestinated the Son of God with power through the Spirit of holiness, by the resurrection from the dead of our Lord Jesus Christ."(2) And again, writing to the Romans about Israel, he says: "Whose are the fathers, and from whom is Christ according to the flesh, who is God over all, blessed for ever."(3) And again, in his Epistle to the Galatians, he says: "But when the fulness of time had come, God sent forth His Son, made of a woman, made under the law, to redeem them that were under the law, that we might receive the adoption; "(4) plainly indicating one God, who did by the prophets make promise of the Son, and one Jesus Christ our Lord, who was of the seed of David according to His birth from Mary; and that Jesus Christ was appointed the Son of God with power, according to the Spirit of holiness, by the resurrection from the dead, as being the first begotten in all the creation;(5) the Son of God being made the Son Of man, that through Him we may receive the adoption,—humanity(6) sustaining, and receiving, and embracing the Son of God. Wherefore Mark also says: "The beginning of the Gospel of Jesus Christ, the Son of God; as it is written in the prophets."(7) Knowing one and the same Son of God, Jesus Christ, who was announced by the prophets, who from the fruit of David's body was Emmanuel, "'the messenger of great counsel of the Father;" through whom God caused the day–spring and the Just One to arise to the house of David, and raised up for him an horn of salvation, "and established a testimony in Jacob;"(9) as David says when discoursing on the causes of His birth: "And He appointed a law in Israel, that another generation might know [Him,] the children which should he born from these, and they arising shall themselves declare to their children, so that they might set their hope in God, and seek after His

commandments."(10) And again, the angel said, when bringing good tidings to Mary: "He shall he great, and shall be called the Son of the Highest; and the Lord shall give unto Him the throne of His father David;"(11) acknowledging that He who is the Son of the Highest, the same is Himself also the Son of David. And David, knowing by the Spirit the dispensation of the advent of this Person, by which He is supreme over all the living and dead, confessed Him as Lord, sitting on the right hand of the Most High Father.(12)

4. But Simeon also—he who had received an intimation from the Holy Ghost that he should not see death, until first he had beheld Christ Jesus—taking Him, the first–begotten of the Virgin, into his hands, blessed God, and said, "Lord, now lettest Thou Thy servant depart in peace, according to Thy word: because mine eyes have seen Thy salvation, which Thou hast prepared before the face of all people; a light to lighten the Gentiles, and the glory of Thy people Israel;"(13) confessing thus, that the infant whom he was holding in his hands, Jesus, born of Mary, was Christ Himself, the Son of God, the light of all, the glory of Israel itself, and the peace and refreshing of those who had fallen asleep. For He was already despoiling men, by removing their ignorance, conferring upon them His own knowledge, and scattering abroad those who recognised Him, as Esaias says: "Call His name, Quickly spoil, Rapidly divide."(1) Now these are the works of Christ. He therefore was Himself Christ, whom Simeon carrying [in his arms] blessed the Most High; on beholding whom the shepherds glorified God; whom John, while yet in his mother's womb, and He (Christ) in that of Mary, recognising as the Lord, saluted with leaping; whom the Magi, when they had seen, adored, and offered their gifts [to Him], as I have already stated, and prostrated themselves to the eternal King, departed by another way, not now returning by the way of the Assyrians. "For before the child shall have knowledge to cry, Father or mother, He shall receive the power of Damascus, and the spoils of Samaria, against the king of the Assyrians;"(2) declaring, in a mysterious manner indeed, but emphatically, that the Lord did fight with a hidden hand against Amalek.(3) For this cause, too, He suddenly removed those children belonging to the house of David, whose happy lot it was to have been born at that time, that He might send them on before into His kingdom; He, since He was Himself an infant, so arranging it that human infants should be martyrs, slain, according to the Scriptures, for the sake of Christ, who was born in Bethlehem of Judah, in the city of David.(4)

5. Therefore did the Lord also say to His disciples after the resurrection, "O thoughtless ones, and slow of heart to believe all that the prophets have spoken! Ought not Christ to have suffered these things, and to enter into His glory?"(5) And again does He say to them: "These are the words which I spoke unto you while I was yet with you, that all things must be fulfilled which were written in the law of Moses, and in the prophets, and in the Psalms, concerning Me. Then opened He their understanding, that they should understand the Scriptures, and said unto them, Thus it is written, and thus it behoved Christ to suffer, and to rise again from the dead, and that repentance for the remission of sins be preached in His name among all nations."(6) Now this is He who was born of Mary; for He says: "The Son of man must suffer many things, and be rejected, and crucified, and on the third day rise again."(7) The Gospel, therefore, knew no other son of man but Him who was of Mary, who also suffered; and no Christ who flew away from Jesus before the passion; but Him who was born it knew as Jesus Christ the Son of God, and that this same suffered and rose again, as John, the disciple of the Lord, verities, saying: "But these are written, that ye might believe that Jesus is the Christ, the Son of God, and that believing ye might have eternal life in His name,"(8)—foreseeing these blasphemous systems which divide the Lord, as far as lies in their power, saying that He was formed of two different substances. For this reason also he has thus testified to us in his Epistle: "Little children, it is the last time; and as ye have heard that Antichrist doth come, now have many antichrists appeared; whereby we know that it is the last time. They went out from us, but they were not of us; for if they had been of us, they would have continued with us: but [they departed], that they might be made manifest that they are not of us. Know ye therefore, that every lie is from without, and is not of the truth. Who is a liar, but he that denieth that Jesus is the Christ? This is Antichrist."(9)

6. But inasmuch as all those before mentioned, although they certainly do with their tongue confess one Jesus Christ, make fools of themselves, thinking one thing and saying another;(10) for their hypotheses vary, as I have already shown, alleging, [as they do,] that one Being suffered and was born, and that this was Jesus; but that there was another who descended upon Him, and that this was Christ, who also ascended again; and they argue, that he who proceeded from the Demiurge, or he who was dispensational, or he who sprang from Joseph, was the Being subject to suffering; but upon the latter there descended from the invisible and ineffable [places] the former, whom they assert to be incomprehensible, invisible, and impassible: they thus wander from the truth, because their doctrine departs from Him who is truly God, being ignorant that His only-begotten Word, who is always present with the human race, united to and mingled with His own

creation, according to the Father's pleasure, and who became flesh, is Himself Jesus Christ our Lord, who did also suffer for us, and rose again on our behalf, and who will come again in the glory of His Father, to raise up all flesh, and for the manifestation of salvation, and to apply the rule of just judgment to all who were made by Him. There is therefore, as I have pointed out, one God the Father, and one Christ Jesus, who came by means of the whole dispensational arrangements [connected with Him], and gath- 443

ered together all things in Himself.(1) But in every respect, too, He is man, the formation of God; and thus He took up man into Himself, the invisible becoming visible, the incomprehensible being made comprehensible, the impassible becoming capable of suffering, and the Word being made man, thus summing up all things in Himself: so that as in super–celestial, spiritual, and invisible things, the Word of God is supreme, so also in things visible and corporeal He might possess the supremacy, and, taking to Himself the pre–eminence, as well as constituting Himself Head of the Church, He might draw all things to Himself at the proper time.

7. With Him is nothing incomplete or out of due season, just as with the Father there is nothing incongruous. For all these things were foreknown by the Father; but the Son works them out at the proper time in perfect order and sequence. This was the reason why, when Mary was urging [Him] on to [perform] the wonderful miracle of the wine, and was desirous before the time to partake(2) of the cup of emblematic significance, the Lord, checking her untimely haste, said, "Woman, what have I to do with thee? mine hour is not yet come"(3)—waiting for that hour which was foreknown by the Father. This is also the reason why, when men were often desirous to take Him, it is said, "No man laid hands upon Him, for the hour of His being taken was not yet come;"(4) nor the time of His passion, which had been foreknown by the Father; as also says the prophet Habakkuk, "By this Thou shalt be known when the years have drawn nigh; Thou shalt be set forth when the time comes; because my soul is disturbed by anger, Thou shalt remember Thy mercy."(5) Paul also says: "But when the fulness of time came, God sent forth His Son."(6) By which is made manifest, that all things which had been foreknown of the Father, our Lord did accomplish in their order, season, and hour, foreknown and fitting, being indeed one and the same, but rich and great. For He fulfils the bountiful and comprehensive will of His Father, inasmuch as He is Himself the Saviour of those who are saved, and the Lord of those who are under authority, and the God of all those things which have been formed, the only–begotten of the Father, Christ who was announced, and the Word of God, who became incarnate when the fulness of time had come, at

which the Son of God had to become the Son of man.

8. All, therefore, are outside of the [Christian] dispensation, who, under pretext of knowledge, understand that Jesus was one, and Christ another, and the Only–begotten another, from whom again is the Word, and that the Saviour is another, whom these disciples of error allege to be a production of those who were made Aeons in a state of degeneracy. Such men are to outward appearance sheep; for they appear to be like us, by what they say in public, repeating the same words as we do; but inwardly they are wolves. Their doctrine is homicidal, conjuring up, as it does, a number of gods, and simulating many Fathers, but lowering and dividing the Son of God in many ways. These are they against whom the Lord has cautioned us beforehand; and His disciple, in his Epistle already mentioned, commands us to avoid them, when he says: "For many deceivers are entered into the world, who confess not that Jesus Christ is come in the flesh. This is a deceiver and an antichrist. Take heed to them, that ye lose not what ye have wrought."(7) And again does he say in the Epistle: "Many false prophets are gone out into the world. Hereby know ye the Spirit of God: Every spirit that confesseth that Jesus Christ is come in the flesh is of God; and every spirit which separates Jesus Christ is not of God, but is of antichrist."(8) These words agree with what was said in the Gospel, that "the Word was made flesh, and dwelt among us." Wherefore he again exclaims in his Epistle, "Every one that believeth that Jesus is the Christ, has been born of God;"(9) knowing Jesus Christ to be one and the same, to whom the gates of heaven were opened, because of His taking upon Him flesh: who shall also come in the same flesh in which He suffered, revealing the glory of the Father.

9. Concurring with these statements, Paul, speaking to the Romans, declares: "Much more they who receive abundance of grace and righteousness for [eternal] life, shall reign by one, Christ Jesus."(10) It follows from this, that he knew nothing of that Christ who flew away from Jesus; nor did he of the Saviour above, whom they hold to be impassible. For if, in truth, the one suffered, and the other remained incapable of suffering, and the one was born, but the other descended upon him who was born, and left him gain, it is not one, but two, that are shown forth. But that the apostle did know Him as one, both who was born and who suffered, namely Christ Jesus, he again says in the same Epistle: "Know ye not, that so many of us as were baptized in Christ Jesus were baptized in His death? that like as Christ rose from the dead, so should we also walk in newness of life."(1) But again, showing that Christ did suffer, and was Himself the Son of God, who died for us, and redeemed us with His blood at the time appointed beforehand, he says:

"For how is it, that Christ, when we were yet without strength, in due time died for the ungodly? But God commendeth His love towards us, in that, while we were yet sinners, Christ died for us. Much more, then, being now justified by His blood, we shall be saved from wrath through Him. For if, when we were enemies, we were reconciled to God by the death of His Son; much more, being reconciled, we shall be saved by His life."(2) He declares in the plainest manner, that the same Being who was laid hold of, and underwent suffering, and shed His blood for us, was both Christ and the Son of God, who did also rise again, and was taken up into heaven, as he himself [Paul] says: "But at the same time, [it, is] Christ [that] died, yea rather, that is risen again, who is even at the fight hand of God."(3) And again, "Knowing that Christ, rising from the dead, dieth no more:"(4) for, as himself foreseeing, through the Spirit, the subdivisions of evil teachers [with regard to the Lord's person], and being desirous of cutting away from them all occasion of cavil, he says what has been already stated, [and also declares:] "But if the Spirit of Him that raised up Jesus from the dead dwell in you, He that raised up Christ from the dead shall also quicken your mortal bodies."(5) This he does not utter to those alone who wish to hear: Do not err, [he says to all:] Jesus Christ, the Son of God, is one and the same, who did by suffering reconcile us to God, and rose from the dead; who is at the right hand of the Father, and perfect in all things; "who, when He was buffeted, struck not in return; who, when He suffered, threatened not;"(6) and when He underwent tyranny, He prayed His Father that He would forgive those who had crucified Him. For He did Himself truly bring in salvation: since He is Himself the Word of God, Himself the Only−begotten of the Father, Christ Jesus our Lord.

CHAP. XVII.—THE APOSTLES TEACH THAT IT WAS NEITHER CHRIST NOR THE SAVIOUR, BUT THE HOLY SPIRIT, WHO DID DESCEND UPON JESUS. THE REASON FOR THIS DESCENT.

1. It certainly was in the power of the apostles to declare that Christ descended upon Jesus, or that the so−called superior Saviour [came down] upon the dispensational one, or he who is from the invisible places upon him from the Demiurge; but they neither knew nor said anything of the kind: for, had they known it, they would have also certainly stated it. But what really was the case, that did they record, [namely,] that the Spirit of God as a dove descended upon Him; this Spirit, of whom it was declared by Isaiah, "And the Spirit of God shall rest upon Him,"(7) as I have already said. And again: "The Spirit

of the Lord is upon Me, because He hath anointed Me."(8) That is the Spirit of whom the Lord declares, "For it is not ye that speak, but the Spirit of your Father which speaketh in you."(9) And again, giving to the disciples the power of regeneration into God,(10) He said to them," Go and teach all nations, baptizing them in the name of the Father, and of the Son, and of the Holy Ghost."(11) For [God] promised, that in the last times He would pour Him [the Spirit] upon [His] servants and handmaids, that they might prophesy; wherefore He did also descend upon the Son of God, made the Son of man, becoming accustomed in fellowship with Him to dwell in the human race, to rest with human beings, and to dwell in the workmanship of God, working the will of the Father in them, and renewing them from their old habits into the newness of Christ.

2. This Spirit did David ask for the human race, saying, "And stablish me with Thine all-governing Spirit;"(12) who also, as Luke says, descended at the day of Pentecost upon the disciples after the Lord's ascension, having power to admit all nations to the entrance of life, and to the opening of the new covenant; from whence also, with one accord in all languages, they uttered praise to God, the Spirit bringing distant tribes to unity, and offering to the Father the first-fruits of all nations. Wherefore also the Lord promised to send the Comforter,(13) who should join us to God. For as a compacted lump of dough cannot be formed of dry wheat without fluid matter, nor can a loaf possess unity, so, in like manner, neither could we, being many, be made one in Christ Jesus without the water from heaven. And as dry earth does not bring forth unless it receive moisture, in like manner we also, being originally a dry tree, could never have brought forth fruit unto life without the voluntary rain from above. For our bodies have received unity among themselves by means of that layer which leads to incorruption; but our souls, by means of the Spirit. Wherefore both are necessary, since both contribute towards the life of God, our Lord compassionating that erring Samaritan woman(1)—who did not remain with one husband, but committed fornication by [contracting] many marriages—by pointing out, and promising to her living water, so that she should thirst no more, nor occupy herself in acquiring the refreshing water obtained by labour, having in herself water springing up to eternal life. The Lord, receiving this as a gift from His Father, does Himself also confer it upon those who are partakers of Himself, sending the Holy Spirit upon all the earth.

3. Gideon,(2) that Israelite whom God chose, that he might save the people of Israel from the power of foreigners, foreseeing this gracious gift, changed his request, and prophesied that there would be dryness upon the fleece of wool (a type of the people), on which

alone at first there had been dew; thus indicating that they should no longer have the Holy Spirit from God, as saith Esaias, "I will also command the clouds, that they rain no rain upon it,"(3) but that the dew, which is the Spirit of God, who descended upon the Lord, should be diffused throughout all the earth, "the spirit of wisdom and understanding, the spirit of counsel and might, the spirit of knowledge and piety, the spirit of the fear of God."(4) This Spirit, again, He did confer upon the Church, sending throughout all the world the Comforter from heaven, from whence also the Lord tells us that the devil, like lightning, was cast down.(5) Wherefore we have need of the dew of God, that we be not consumed by fire, nor be rendered unfruitful, and that where we have an accuser there we may have also an Advocate,(6) the Lord commending to the Holy Spirit His own man,(7) who had fallen among thieves,(8) whom He Himself compassionated, and bound up his wounds, giving two royal denaria; so that we, receiving by the Spirit the image and superscription of the Father and the Son, might cause the denarium entrusted to us to be fruitful, counting out the increase [thereof] to the Lord.(9)

4. The Spirit, therefore, descending under the predestined dispensation, and the Son of God, the Only-begotten, who is also the Word of the Father, coming in the fulness of time, having become incarnate in man for the sake of man, and fulfilling all the conditions of human nature, our Lord Jesus Christ being one and the same, as He Himself the Lord doth testify, as the apostles confess, and as the prophets announce,—all the doctrines of these men who have invented putative Ogdoads and Tetrads, and imagined subdivisions [of the Lord's person], have been proved falsehoods. These(10) men do, in fact, set the Spirit aside altogether; they understand that Christ was one and Jesus another; and they teach that there was not one Christ, but many. And if they speak of them as united, they do again separate them: for they show that one did indeed undergo sufferings, but that the other remained impassible; that the one truly did ascend to the Pleroma, but the other remained in the intermediate place; that the one does truly feast and revel in places invisible and above all name, but that the other is seated with the Demiurge, emptying him of power. It will therefore be incumbent upon thee, and all others who give their attention to this writing, and are anxious about their own salvation, not readily to express acquiescence when they hear abroad the speeches of these men: for, speaking things resembling the [doctrine of the] faithful, as I have already observed, not only do they hold opinions which are different, but absolutely contrary, and in all points full of blasphemies, by which they destroy those persons who, by reason of the resemblance of the words, imbibe a poison which disagrees with their constitution, just as if one, giving lime mixed with water for milk, should mislead by the similitude of the

colour; as a man" superior to me has said, concerning all that in any way corrupt the things of God and adulterate the truth, "Lime is wickedly mixed with the milk of God."

CHAP. XVIII.—CONTINUATION OF THE FOREGOING ARGUMENT. PROOFS FROM THE WRITINGS OF ST. PAUL, AND FROM THE WORDS OF OUR LORD, THAT CHRIST AND JESUS CANNOT BE CONSIDERED AS DISTINCT BEINGS; NEITHER CAN IT BE ALLEGED THAT THE SON OF GOD BECAME MAN MERELY IN APPEARANCE, BUT THAT HE DID SO TRULY AND ACTUALLY.

1.(12) As it has been clearly demonstrated that the Word, who existed in the beginning with God, by whom all things were made, who was also always present with mankind, was in these last days, according to the time appointed by the Father, united to His own workmanship, inasmuch as He became a man liable to suffering, [it follows] that every objection is set aside of those who say, "If our Lord was born at that time, Christ had therefore no previous existence." For I have shown that the Son of God did not then begin to exist, being with the Father from the beginning; but when He became incarnate, and was made man, He commenced afresh(1) the long line of human beings, and furnished us, in a brief, comprehensive manner, with salvation; so that what we had lost in Adam—namely, to be according to the image and likeness of God—that we might recover in Christ Jesus.

2. For as it was not possible that the man who had once for all been conquered, and who had been destroyed through disobedience, could reform himself, and obtain the prize of victory; and as it was also impossible that he could attain to salvation who had fallen under the power of sin,—the Son effected both these things, being the Word of God, descending from the Father, becoming incarnate, stooping low, even to death, and consummating the arranged plan of our salvation, upon whom [Paul], exhorting us unhesitatingly to believe, again says, "Who shall ascend into heaven? that is, to bring down Christ; or who shall descend into the deep? that is, to liberate Christ again from the dead."(2) Then he continues, "If thou shalt confess with thy mouth the Lord Jesus, and shalt believe in thine heart that God hath raised Him from the dead, thou shalt be saved."(3) And he renders the reason why the Son of God did these things, saying, "For

to this end Christ both lived, and died, and revived, that He might rule over the living and the dead."(4) And again, writing to the Corinthians, he declares, "But we preach Christ Jesus crucified;"(5) and adds, "The cup of blessing which we bless, is it not the communion of the blood of Christ?"(6)

3. But who is it that has had fellowship with us in the matter of food? Whether is it he who is conceived of by them as the Christ above, who extended himself through Horos, and imparted a form to their mother; or is it He who is from the Virgin, Emmanuel, who did eat butter and honey,(7) of whom the prophet declared, "He is also a man, and who shall know him?"(8) He was likewise preached by Paul: "For I delivered," he says, "unto you first of all, that Christ died for our sins, according to the Scriptures; and that He was buried, and rose again the third day, according to the Scriptures."(9) It is plain, then, that Paul knew no other Christ besides Him alone, who both suffered, and was buried, and rose gain, who was also born, and whom he speaks of as man. For after remarking, "But if Christ be preached, that He rose from the dead,"(10) he continues, rendering the reason of His incarnation, "For since by man came death, by man [came] also the resurrection of the dead." And everywhere, when [referring to] the passion of our Lord, and to His human nature, and His subjection to death, he employs the name of Christ, as in that passage: "Destroy not him with thy meat for whom Christ died."(11) And again: "But now, in Christ, ye who sometimes were far off are made nigh by the blood of Christ."(12) And again: "Christ has redeemed us from the curse of the law, being made a curse for us: for it is written, Cursed is every one that hangeth upon a tree."(13) And again: "And through thy knowledge shall the weak brother perish, for whom Christ died;"(14) indicating that the impassible Christ did not descend upon Jesus, but that He Himself, because He was Jesus Christ, suffered for us; He, who lay in the tomb, and rose again, who descended and ascended,—the Son of God having been made the Son of man, as the very name itself doth declare. For in the name of Christ is implied, He that anoints, He that is anointed, and the unction itself with which He is anointed. And it is the Father who anoints, but the Son who is anointed by the Spirit, who is the unction, as the Word declares by Isaiah, "The Spirit of the Lord is upon me, because He hath anointed me,"(15)—pointing out both the anointing Father, the anointed Son, and the unction, which is the Spirit.

4. The Lord Himself, too, makes it evident who it was that suffered; for when He asked the disciples, "Who do men say that I, the Son of man, am?"(16) and when Peter had replied, "Thou art the Christ, the Son of the living God;" and when he had been

commended by Him [in these words], "That flesh and blood had not revealed it to him, but the Father who is in heaven," He made it clear that He, the Son of man, is Christ the Son of the living God. "For from that time forth," it is said, "He began to show to His disciples, how that He must go unto Jerusalem, and suffer many things of the priests, and be rejected, and crucified, and rise again the third day."(1) He who was acknowledged by Peter as Christ, who pronounced him blessed because the Father had revealed the Son of the living God to him, said that He must Himself suffer many things, and be crucified; and then He rebuked Peter, who imagined that He was the Christ as the generality of men supposed(2) [that the Christ should be], and was averse to the idea of His suffering, [and] said to the disciples, "If any man will come after Me, let him deny himself, and take up his cross, and follow Me. For whosoever will save his life, shall lose it; and whosoever will lose it for My sake shall save it."(3) For these things Christ spoke openly, He being Himself the Saviour of those who should be delivered over to death for their confession of Him, and lose their lives.

5. If, however, He was Himself not to suffer, but should fly away from Jesus, why did He exhort His disciples to take up the cross and follow Him,—that cross which these men represent Him as not having taken up, but [speak of Him] as having relinquished the dispensation of suffering? For that He did not say this with reference to the acknowledging of the Stauros (cross) above, as some among them venture to expound, but with respect to the suffering which He should Himself undergo, and that His disciples should endure, He implies when He says, "For whosoever will save his life, shall lose it; and whosoever will lose, shall find it. And that His disciples must suffer for His sake, He [implied when He] said to the Jews, "Behold, I send you prophets, and wise men, and scribes: and some of them ye shall kill and crucify."(4) And to the disciples He was wont to say, "And ye shall stand before governors and kings for My sake; and they shall scourge some of you, and slay you, and persecute you from city to city."(5) He knew, therefore, both those who should suffer persecution, and He knew those who should have to be scourged and slain because of Him; and He did not speak of any other cross, but of the suffering which He should Himself undergo first, and His disciples afterwards. For this purpose did He give them this exhortation: "Fear not them which kill the body, but are not able to kill the soul; but rather fear Him who is able to send both soul and body into hell;"(6) [thus exhorting them] to hold fast those professions of faith which they had made in reference to Him. For He promised to confess before His Father those who should confess His name before men; but declared that He

would deny those who should deny Him, and would be ashamed of those who should be ashamed to confess Him. And although these things are so, some of these men have proceeded to such a degree of temerity, that they even pour contempt upon the martyrs, and vituperate those who are slain on account of the confession of the Lord, and who suffer all things predicted by the Lord, and who in this respect strive to follow the footprints of the Lord's passion, having become martyrs of the suffering One; these we do also enrol with the martyrs themselves. For, when inquisition shall be made for their blood,(7) and they shall attain to glory, then all shall be confounded by Christ, who have cast a slur upon their martyrdom. And from this fact, that He exclaimed upon the cross, "Father, forgive them, for they know not what they do,"(8) the long−suffering, patience, compassion, and goodness of Christ are exhibited, since He both suffered, and did Himself exculpate those who had maltreated Him. For the Word of God, who said to us, "Love your enemies, and pray for those that hate you,"(9) Himself did this very thing upon the cross; loving the human race to such a degree, that He even prayed for those putting Him to death. If, however, any one, going upon the supposition that there are two[Christs], forms a judgment in regard to them, that [Christ] shall be found much the better one, and more patient, and the truly good one, who, in the midst of His own wounds and stripes, and the other [cruelties] inflicted upon Him, was beneficent, and unmindful of the wrongs perpetrated upon Him, than he who flew away, and sustained neither injury nor insult.

6. This also does likewise meet [the case] of those who maintain that He suffered only in appearance. For if He did not truly suffer, no thanks to Him, since there was no suffering at all; and when we shall actually begin to suffer, He will seem as leading us astray, exhorting us to endure buffering, and to turn the other(10) cheek, if He did not Himself before us in reality suffer the same; and as He misled them by seeming to them what He was not, so does He also mislead us, by exhorting us to endure what He did not endure Himself. [In that case] we shall be even above the Master, because we suffer and sustain what our Master never bore or endured. But as our Lord is alone truly Master, so the Son of God is truly good and patient, the Word of God the Father having been made the Son of man. For He fought and conquered; for He was man contending for the fathers,(11) and through obedience doing away with disobedience completely: for He bound the strong man,(1) and set free the weak, and endowed His own handiwork with salvation, by destroying sin. For He is a most holy and merciful Lord, and loves the human race.

7. Therefore, as I have already said, He caused man (human nature) to cleave to and to become, one with God. For unless man had overcome the enemy of man, the enemy would not have been legitimately vanquished. And again: unless it had been God who had freely given salvation, we could never have possessed it securely. And unless man had been joined to God, he could never have become a partaker of incorruptibility. For it was incumbent upon the Mediator between God and men, by His relationship to both, to bring both to friendship and concord, and present man to God, while He revealed God to man.(2) For, in what way could we be partaken of the adoption of sons, unless we had received from Him through the Son that fellowship which refers to Himself, unless His Word, having been made flesh, had entered into communion with us? Wherefore also He passed through every stage of life, restoring to all communion with God. Those, therefore, who assert that He appeared putatively, and was neither born in the flesh nor truly made man, are as yet under the old condemnation, holding out patronage to sin; for, by their showing, death has not been vanquished, which "reigned from Adam to Moses, even over them that had not sinned after the similitude of Adam's transgression."(3) But the law coming, which was given by Moses, and testifying of sin that it is a sinner, did truly take away his (death's) kingdom, showing that he was no king, but a robber; and it revealed him as a murderer. It laid, however, a weighty burden upon man, who had sin in himself, showing that he was liable to death. For as the law was spiritual, it merely made sin to stand out in relief, but did not destroy it. For sin had no dominion over the spirit, but over man. For it behoved Him who was to destroy sin, and redeem man under the power of death, that He should Himself be made that very same thing which he was, that is, man; who had been drawn by sin into bondage, but was held by death, so that sin should be destroyed by man, and man should go forth from death. For as by the disobedience of the one man who was originally moulded from virgin soil, the many were made sinners,(4) and forfeited life; so was it necessary that, by the obedience of one man,

who was originally born from a virgin, many should be justified and receive salvation. Thus, then, was the Word of God made man, as also Moses says: "God, true are His works."(5) But if, not having been made flesh, He did appear as if flesh, His work was not a true one. But what He did appear, that He also was: God recapitulated in Himself the ancient formation of man, that He might kill sin, deprive death of its power, and vivify man; and therefore His works are true.

CHAP. XIX.—JESUS CHRIST WAS NOT A MERE MAN, BEGOTTEN FROM JOSEPH IN THE ORDINARY COURSE OF NATURE, BUT WAS VERY GOD, BEGOTTEN OF THE FATHER MOST HIGH, AND VERY MAN, BORN' OF THE VIRGIN.

1. But again, those who assert that He was simply a mere man, begotten by Joseph, remaining in the bondage of the old disobedience, are in a state of death having been not as yet joined to the Word of God the Father, nor receiving liberty through the Son, as He does Himself declare: "If the Son shall make you free, ye shall be free indeed."(6) But, being ignorant of Him who from the Virgin is Emmanuel, they are deprived of His gift, which is eternal life;(7) and not receiving the incorruptible Word, they remain in mortal flesh, and are debtors to death, not obtaining the antidote of life. To whom the Word says, mentioning His own gift of grace: "I said, Ye are all the sons of the Highest, and gods; but ye shall die like men."(8) He speaks undoubtedly these words to those who have not received the gift of adoption, but who despise the incarnation of the pure generation of the Word of God,(9) defraud human nature of promotion into God, and prove themselves ungrateful to the Word of God, who became flesh for them. For it was for this end that the Word of God was made man, and He who was the Son of God became the Son of man, that man, having been taken into the Word, and receiving the adoption, might become the son of God. For by no other means could we have attained to incorruptibility and immortality, unless we had been united to incorruptibility and immortality. But how could we be joined to incorruptibility and immortality, unless, first, incorruptibility and immortality had become that which we also are, so that the corruptible might be swallowed up by incorruptibility, and the mortal by immortality, that might receive the adoption of sons?

2. For this reason [it is ,said], "Who shall declare His generation?"(1) since "He is a man, and who shall recognise Him?"(2) But he to whom the Father which is in heaven has revealed Him,(3) knows Him, so that he understands that He who "was not born either by the will of the flesh, or by the will of man,"(4) is the Son of man, this is Christ, the Son of the living God. For I have shown from the Scriptures,(5) that no one of the sons of Adam is as to everything, and absolutely, called God, or named Lord. But that He is Himself in His own right, beyond all men who ever lived, God, and Lord, and King Eternal, and the

Incarnate Word, proclaimed by all the prophets, the apostles, and by the Spirit Himself, may be seen by all who have attained to even a small portion of the truth. Now, the Scriptures would not have testified these things of Him, if, like others, He had been a mere man. But that He had, beyond all others, in Himself that pre−eminent birth which is from the Most High Father, and also experienced that pre−eminent generation which is from the Virgin,(6) the divine Scriptures do in both respects testify of Him: also, that He was a man without comeliness, and liable to suffering;(7) that He sat upon the foal of an ass;(8) that He received for drink, vinegar and gall;(9) that He was despised among the people, and humbled Himself even to death and that He is the holy Lord, the Wonderful, the Counsellor, the Beautiful in appearance, and the Mighty God,(10) coming on the clouds as the Judge of all men;(11)—all these things did the Scriptures prophesy of Him.

3. For as He became man in order to undergo temptation, so also was He the Word that He might be glorified; the Word remaining quiescent, that He might be capable of being tempted, dishonoured, crucified, and of suffering death, but the human nature being swallowed up in it (the divine), when it conquered, and endured [without yielding], and performed acts of kindness, and rose again, and was received up [into heaven]. He therefore, the Son of God, our Lord, being the Word of the Father, and the Son of man, since He had a generation as to His human nature from Mary—who was descended from mankind, and who was herself a

human being—was made the Son of man.(12) Wherefore also the Lord Himself gave us a sign, in the depth below, and in the height above, which man did not ask for, because he never expected that a virgin could conceive, or that it was possible that one remaining a virgin could bring forth a son, and that what was thus born should be" God with us," and descend to those things which are of the earth beneath, seeking the sheep which had perished, which was indeed His own peculiar handiwork, and ascend to the height above, offering and commending to His Father that human nature (hominem) which had been found, making in His own person the first−fruits of the resurrection of man; that, as the Head rose from the dead, so also the remaining pan of the body—[namely, the body] of every man who is found in life—when the time is fulfilled of that condemnation which existed by reason of disobedience, may arise, blended together and strengthened through means of joints and bands(13) by the increase of God, each of the members having its own proper and fit position in the body. For there are many mansions in the Father's house,(14) inasmuch as there are also many members in the body.

CHAP. XX.—GOD SHOWED HIMSELF, BY THE FALL OF MAN, AS PATIENT, BENIGN, MERCIFUL, MIGHTY TO SAVE. MAN IS THEREFORE MOST UNGRATEFUL, IF, UNMINDFUL OF HIS OWN LOT, AND OF THE BENEFITS HELD OUT TO HIM, HE DO NOT ACKNOWLEDGE DIVINE GRACE.

1. Long—suffering therefore was God, when man became a defaulter, as foreseeing that victory which should be granted to him through the Word. For, when strength was made perfect in weakness,(15) it showed the kindness and transcendent power of God. For as He patiently suffered Jonah to be swallowed by the whale, not that he should be swallowed up and perish altogether, but that, having been cast out again, he might be the more subject to God, and might glorify Him the more who had conferred upon him such an unhoped—for deliverance, and might bring the Ninevites to a lasting repentance, so that they should be convened to the Lord, who would deliver them from death, having been struck with awe by that portent which had been wrought in Jonah's case, as the Scripture says of them, "And they returned each from his evil way, and the unrighteousness which was in their hands, saying, Who knoweth if God will repent, and turn away His anger from us, and we shall not perish?"(16)—so also, from the beginning, did God permit man to be swallowed up by the great whale, who was the author of transgression, not that he should perish altogether when so engulphed; but, arranging and preparing the plan of salvation, which was accomplished by the Word, through the sign of Jonah, for those who held the same opinion as Jonah regarding the Lord, and who confessed, and said, "I am a servant of the Lord, and I worship the Lord God of heaven, who hath made the sea and the dry land."(1) [This was done] that man, receiving an unhoped—for salvation from God, might rise from the dead, and glorify God, and repeat that word which was uttered in prophecy by Jonah: "I cried by reason of mine affliction to the Lord my God, and He heard me out of the belly of hell;"(2) and that he might always continue glorifying God, and giving thanks without ceasing, for that salvation which he has derived from Him, "that no flesh should glory in the Lord's presence;"(3) and that man should never adopt an opposite opinion with regard to God, supposing that the incorruptibility which belongs to him is his own naturally, and by thus not holding the truth, should boast with empty superciliousness, as if he were naturally like to God. For he (Satan) thus rendered him (man) more ungrateful towards his Creator, obscured the

love which God had towards man, and blinded his mind not to perceive what is worthy of God, comparing himself with, and judging himself equal to, God.

2. This, therefore, was the [object of the] long–suffering of God, that man, passing through all things, and acquiring the knowledge of moral discipline, then attaining to the resurrection from the dead, and learning by experience what is the source of his deliverance, may always live in a state of gratitude to the Lord, having obtained from Him the gift of incorruptibility, that he might love Him the more; for "he to whom more is forgiven, loveth more:"(4) and that he may know himself, how mortal and weak he is; while he also understands respecting God, that He is immortal and powerful to such a degree as to confer immortality upon what is mortal, and eternity upon what is temporal; and may understand also the other attributes of God displayed towards himself, by means of which being instructed he may think of God in accordance with the divine greatness. For the glory of man [is] God, but [His] works [are the glory] of God; and the receptacle of all His. wisdom and power [is] man. Just as the physician is proved by his patients, so is God also revealed through men. And therefore Paul declares, "For God hath concluded all in unbelief,

that He may have mercy upon all;"(5) not saying this in reference to spiritual Aeons, but to man, who had been disobedient to God, and being cast off from immortality, then obtained mercy, receiving through the Son of God that adoption which is [accomplished] by Himself. For he who holds, without pride and boasting, the true glory (opinion) regarding created things and the Creator, who is the Almighty God of all, and who has granted existence to all; [such an one,] continuing in His love(6) and subjection, and giving of thanks, shall also receive from Him the greater glory of promotion,(7) looking forward to the time when he shall become like Him who died for him, for He, too, "was made in the likeness of sinful flesh,"(8) to condemn sin, and to cast it, as now a condemned thing, away beyond the flesh, but that He might call man forth into His own likeness, assigning him as [His own] imitator to God, and imposing on him His Father's law, in order that he may see God, and granting him power to receive the Father; [being](9) the Word of God who dwelt in man, and became the Son of man, that He might accustom man to receive God, and God to dwell in man, according to the good pleasure of the Father.

3. On this account, therefore, the Lord Himself,(10) who is Emmanuel from the Virgin,(11) is the sign of our salvation, since it was the Lord Himself who saved them,

because they could not be saved by their own instrumentality; and, therefore, when Paul sets forth human infirmity, he says: "For I know that there dwelleth in my flesh no good thing,"(12) showing that the "good thing" of our salvation is not from us, but from God. And again: "Wretched man that I am, who shall deliver me from the body of this death?"(13) Then he introduces the Deliverer, [saying,] "The grace of Jesus Christ our Lord." And Isaiah declares this also, [when he says:] "Be ye strengthened, ye hands that hang down, and ye feeble knees; be ye encouraged, ye feeble-minded; be comforted, fear not: behold, our God has given judgment with retribution, and shall recompense: He will come Himself, and will save us."(14) Here we see, that not by ourselves, but by the help of God, we must be saved.

4. Again, that it should not be a mere man who should save us, nor [one] without flesh—for the angels are without flesh—[the same prophet] announced, saying: "Neither an eider,(1) nor angel, but the Lord Himself will save them because He loves them, and will spare them He will Himself set them free."(2) And that He should Himself become very man, visible, when He should be the Word giving salvation, Isaiah again sap: "Behold, city of Zion: thine eyes shall see our salvation."(3) And that it was not a mere man who died for us, Isaiah says: "And the holy Lord remembered His dead Israel, who had slept in the land of sepulture; and He came down to preach His salvation to them, that He might save them."(4) And Amos (Micah) the prophet declares the same: "He will turn again, and will have compassion upon us: He will destroy our iniquities, and will cast our sins into the depths of the sea."(5) And again, specifying the place of His advent, he says: "The Lord hath spoken from Zion, and He has uttered His voice from Jerusalem."(6) And that it is from that region which is towards the south of the inheritance of Judah that the Son of God shall come, who is God, and who was from Bethlehem, where the Lord was born [and] will send out His praise through all the earth, thus(7) says the prophet Habakkuk: "God shall come from the south, and the Holy One from Mount, Effrem. His power covered the heavens over, and the earth is full of His praise. Before His face shall go forth the Word, and His feet shall advance in the plains."(8) Thus he indicates in clear terms that He is God, and that His advent was [to take place] in Bethlehem, and from Mount Effrem, which is towards the south of the inheritance, and that [He is] man. For he says, "His feet shall advance in the plains:" and this is an indication proper to man.(9)

CHAP. XXI.—A VINDICATION OF THE PROPHECY IN ISAIAH (VII. 14) AGAINST THE MISINTERPRETATIONS OF THEODOTION, AQUILA, THE EBIONITES, AND THE JEWS. AUTHORITY OF THE SEPTUAGINT VERSION. ARGUMENTS IN PROOF THAT CHRIST WAS BORN OF A VIRGIN.

1. God, then, was made man, and the Lord did Himself save us, giving us the token of the

Virgin. But not as some allege, among those now presuming to expound the Scripture, [thus:] "Behold, a young woman shall conceive, and bring forth a son,"(10) as Theodotion the Ephesian has interpreted, and Aquila of Pontus,(11) both Jewish proselytes. The Ebionites, following these, assert that He was begotten by Joseph; thus destroying, as far as in them lies, such a marvellous dispensation of God, and setting aside the testimony of the prophets which proceeded from God. For truly this prediction was uttered before the removal of the people to Babylon; that is, anterior to the supremacy acquired by the Medes and Persians. But it was interpreted into Greek by the Jews themselves, much before the period of our Lord's advent, that there might remain no suspicion that perchance the Jews, complying with our humour, did put this interpretation upon these words. They indeed, had they been cognizant of our future existence, and that we should use these proofs from the Scriptures, would themselves never have hesitated to burn their own Scriptures, which do declare that all other nations partake of [eternal] life, and show that they who boast themselves as being the house of Jacob and the people of Israel, am disinherited from the grace of God.

2. For before the Romans possessed their kingdom,(12) while as yet the Macedonians held Asia, Ptolemy the son of Lagus, being anxious to adorn the library which he had founded in Alexandria, with a collection of the writings of all men, which were [works] of merit, made request to the people of Jerusalem, that they should have their Scriptures translated into the Greek language. And they—for at that time they were still subject to the Macedonians—sent to Ptolemy seventy of their elders, who were thoroughly skilled in the Scriptures and in both the languages, to carry out what he had desired.(13) But he, wishing to test them individually, and fearing lest they might perchance, by taking counsel together, conceal the truth in the Scriptures, by their interpretation, separated them from each other, and commanded them all to write the same translation. He did this

with respect to all the books. But when they came together in the same place before Ptolemy, and each of them compared his own interpretation with that of every other, God was indeed glorified, and the Scriptures were acknowledged as truly divine. For all of them read out the common translation [which they had prepared] in the very same words and the very same names, from beginning to end, so that even the Gentiles present perceived that the Scriptures had been interpreted by the inspiration of God.(1) And there was nothing astonishing in God having done this,—He who, when, during the captivity of the people under Nebuchadnezzar, the Scriptures had been corrupted, and when, after seventy years, the Jews had returned to their own land, then, in the times of Artaxerxes king of the Persians, inspired Esdras the priest, of the tribe of Levi, to recast(2) all the words of the former prophets, and to re-establish with the people the Mosaic legislation.

3. Since, therefore, the Scriptures have been interpreted with such fidelity, and by the grace of God, and since from these God has prepared and formed again our faith towards His Son, and has preserved to us the unadulterated Scriptures in Egypt, where the house of Jacob flourished, fleeing from the famine in Canaan; where also our Lord was preserved when He fled from the persecution set on foot by Herod; and [since] this interpretation of these Scriptures was made prior to our Lord's descent [to earth], and came into being before the Christians appeared—for our Lord was bern about the forty-first year of the reign of Augustus; but Ptolemy was much earlier, under whom the Scriptures were interpreted;—[since these things are so, I say,] truly these men are proved to be impudent and presumptuous, who would now show a desire to make different translations, when we refute them out of these Scriptures, and shut them up to a belief in the advent of the Son of God. But our faith is stedfast, unfeigned, and the only true one, having clear proof from these Scriptures, which were interpreted in the way I have related; and the preaching of the Church is without interpolation. For the apostles, since they are of more ancient date than all these [heretics], agree with this aforesaid translation; and the translation harmonizes with the tradition of the apostles. For Peter, and John, and Matthew, and Paul, and the rest successively, as well as their followers, did set forth all prophetical [announce-merits], just as(3) the interpretation of the elders contains them.

4. For the one and the same Spirit of God, who proclaimed by the prophets what and of what sort the advent of the Lord should be, did by these elders give a just interpretation of what had been truly prophesied; and He did Himself, by the apostles, announce that the fulness of the times of the adoption had arrived, that the kingdom of heaven had drawn

nigh, and that He was dwelling within those that believe on Him who was born Emmanuel of the Virgin. To this effect they testify, [saying,] that before Joseph had come together with Mary, while she therefore remained in virginity, "she was found with child of the Holy Ghost;"(4) and that the angel Gabriel said unto her, "The Holy Ghost shall come upon thee, and the power of the Highest shall overshadow thee; therefore also that holy thing which shall be born of thee shall be called the Son of God;"(5) and that the angel said to Joseph in a dream, "Now this was done, that it might be fulfilled which was spoken by Isaiah the prophet, Behold, a virgin shall be with child."(6) But the elders have thus interpreted what Esaias said: "And the Lord, moreover, said unto Ahaz, Ask for thyself a sign from the Lord thy God out of the depth below, or from the height above. And Ahaz said, I will not ask, and I will not tempt the Lord. And he said, It is not a small thing(7) for you to weary men; and how does the Lord weary them? Therefore the Lord himself shall give you a sign; Behold, a virgin shall conceive, and bear a son; and ye shall call His name Emmanuel. Butter and honey shall He eat: before He knows or chooses out things that are evil, He shall exchange them for what is good; for before the child knows good or evil, He shall not consent to evil, that He may choose that which is good."(8) Carefully, then, has the Holy Ghost pointed out, by what has been said, His birth from a virgin, and His essence, that He is God (for the name Emmanuel indicates this). And He shows that He is a man, when He says, "Butter and honey shall He eat;" and in that He terms Him a child also, [in saying,] "before He knows good and evil;" for these are all the tokens of a human infant. But that He "will not consent to evil, that He may choose that which is good,"—this is proper to God; that by the fact, that He shall eat butter and honey, we should not understand that He is a mere man only, nor, on the other hand, from the name Emmanuel, should suspect Him to be God without flesh.

5. And when He says, "Hear, O house of David,"(9) He performed the part of one indicating that He whom God promised David that He would raise up from the fruit of his belly (ventris) an eternal King, is the same who was born of the Virgin, herself of the lineage of David. For on this account also, He promised that the King should be "of the fruit of his belly," which was the appropriate [term to use with respect] to a virgin conceiving, and not "of the fruit of his loins," nor "of the fruit of his reins," which expression is appropriate to a generating man, and a woman conceiving by a man. In this promise, therefore, the Scripture excluded all virile influence; yet it certainly is not mentioned that He who was born was not from the will of man. But it has fixed and established "the fruit of the belly," that it might declare the generation of Him who should be [born] from the Virgin, as Elisabeth testified when filled with the Holy Ghost, saying

to Mary, "Blessed art thou among women, and blessed is the fruit of thy belly;"(1) the Holy Ghost pointing out to those willing to hear, that the promise which God had made, of raising up a King from the fruit of [David's] belly, was fulfilled in the birth from the Virgin, that is, from Mary. Let those, therefore, who alter the passage of Isaiah thus, "Behold, a young woman shall conceive," and who will have Him to be Joseph's son, also alter the form of the promise which was given to David, when God promised him to raise up, from the fruit of his belly, the horn of Christ the King. But they did not understand, otherwise they would have presumed to alter even this passage also.

6. But what Isaiah said, "From the height above, or from the depth beneath,"(2) was meant to indicate, that "He who descended was the same also who ascended."(3) But in this that he said, "The Lord Himself shall give you a sign," he declared an unlooked-for thing with regard to His generation, which could have been accomplished in no other way than by God the Lord of all, God Himself giving a sign in the house of David. For what great thing or what sign should have been in this, that a young woman conceiving by a man should bring forth,—a thing which happens to all women that produce offspring? But since an unlooked-for salvation was to be provided for men through the help of God, so also was the unlooked-for birth from a virgin accomplished; God giving this sign, but man not working it out.

7. On this account also, Daniel,(4) foreseeing His advent, said that a stone, cut out without hands, came into this world. For this is what "without hands" means, that His coming into

this world was not by the operation of human hands, that is, of those men who are accustomed to stone-cutting; that is, Joseph taking no part with regard to it, but Mary alone co-operating with the pre-arranged plan. For this stone from the earth derives existence from both the power and the wisdom of God. Wherefore also Isaiah says: "Thus saith the Lord, Behold, I deposit in the foundations of Zion a stone, precious, elect, the chief, the corner-one, to be had in honour."(5) So, then, we understand that His advent in human nature was not by the will of a man, but by the will of God.

8. Wherefore also Moses giving a type, cast his rod upon the earth,(6) in order that it, by becoming flesh, might expose and swallow up all the opposition of the Egyptians, which was lifting itself up against the pre-arranged plan of God;(7) that the Egyptians themselves might testify that it is the finger of God which works salvation for the people,

and not the son of Joseph. For if He were the son of Joseph, how could He be greater than Solomon, of greater than Jonah,(8) or greater than David,(9) when He was generated from the same seed, and was a descendant of these men? And how was it that He also pronounced Peter blessed, because he acknowledged Him to be the Son of the living God ?(10)

9. But besides, if indeed He had been the son of Joseph, He could not, according to Jeremiah, be either king or heir. For Joseph is shown to be the son of Joachim and Jechoniah, as also Matthew sets forth in his pedigree.(11) But Jechoniah, and all his posterity, were disinherited from the kingdom; Jeremiah thus declaring, "As I live, saith the Lord, if Jechoniah the son of Joachim king of Judah had been made the signet of my right hand, I would pluck him thence, and deliver him into the hand of those seeking thy life."(12) And again: "Jechoniah is dishonoured as a useless vessel, for he has been cast into a land which he knew not. Earth, hear the word of the Lord: Write this man a disinherited person; for none of his seed, sitting on the throne of David, shall prosper, or be a prince in Judah."(13) And again, God speaks of Joachim his father: "Therefore thus saith the Lord concerning Joachim his father, king of Judea, There shall be from him none sitting upon the throne of David: and his dead body shall be cast out in the heat of day, and in the frost of night. And I will look upon him, and upon his sons, and will bring upon them, and upon the inhabitants of Jerusalem, upon the land of Judah, all the evils that I have pronounced against them."(1) Those, therefore, who say that He was begotten of Joseph, and that they have hope in Him, do cause themselves to be disinherited from the kingdom, failing tinder the curse and rebuke directed against Jechoniah and his seed. Because for this reason have these things been spoken concerning Jechoniah, the [Holy] Spirit foreknowing the doctrines of the evil teachers; that they may learn that from his seed—that is, from Joseph—He was not to be born but that, according to the promise of God, from David's belly the King eternal is raised up, who sums up all things in Himself, and has gathered into Himself the ancient formation [of man].(2)

10. For as by one man's disobedience sin entered, and death obtained [a place] through sin; so also by the obedience of one man, righteousness having been introduced, shall cause life to fructify in those persons who in times past were dead.(3) And as the protoplast himself Adam, had his substance from untilled and as yet virgin soil ("for God had not yet sent rain, and man had not tilled the ground"(4)), and was formed by the hand of God, that is, by the Word of God, for "all things were made by Him,"(5) and the Lord took dust from the earth and formed man; so did He who is the Word, recapitulating

Adam in Himself, rightly receive a birth, enabling Him to gather up Adam [into Himself], from Mary, who was as yet a virgin. If, then, the first Adam had a man for his father, and was born of human seed, it were reasonable to say that the second Adam was begotten of Joseph. But if the former was taken from the dust, and God was his Maker, it was incumbent that the latter also, making a recapitulation in Himself, should be formed as man by God, to have an analogy with the former as respects His origin. Why, then, did not God again take dust, but wrought so that the formation should be made of Mary? It was that there might not be another formation called into being, nor any other which should [require to] be saved, but that the very same formation should be summed up [in Christ as had existed in Adam], the analogy having been preserved.

CHAP. XXII.—CHRIST ASSUMED ACTUAL FLESH, CONCEIVED AND BORN OF THE VIRGIN.

1. Those, therefore, who allege that He took nothing from the Virgin do greatly err, [since,] in order that they may cast away the inheritance of the flesh, they also reject the analogy [between Him and Adam]. For if the one [who sprang] from the earth had indeed formation and substance from both the hand and workmanship of God, but the other not from the hand and workmanship of God, then He who was made after the image and likeness of the former did not, in that case, preserve the analogy of man, and He must seem an inconsistent piece of work, not having wherewith He may show His wisdom. But this is to say, that He also appeared putatively as man when He was not man, and that He was made man while taking nothing from man. For if He did not receive the substance of flesh from a human being, He neither was made man nor the Son of man; and if He was not made what we were, He did no great thing in what He suffered and endured. But every one will allow that we are [composed of] a body taken from the earth, and a soul receiving spirit from God. This, therefore, the Word of God was made, recapitulating in Himself His own handiwork; and on this account does He confess Himself the Son of man, and blesses "the meek, because they shall inherit the earth."(6) The Apostle Paul, moreover, in the Epistle to the Galatians, declares plainly, "God sent His Son, made of a woman."(7) And again, in that to the Romans, he says, "Concerning His Son, who was made of the seed of David according to the flesh, who was predestinated as the Son of God with power, according to the spirit of holiness, by the resurrection from the dead, Jesus Christ our Lord."(8)

2.(9) Superfluous, too, in that case is His descent into Mary; for why did He come down into her if He were to take nothing of her? Still further, if He had taken nothing of Mary, He would never have availed Himself of those kinds of food which are derived from the earth, by which that body which has been taken from the earth is nourished; nor would He have hungered, fasting those forty days, like Moses and Elias, unless His body was craving after its own proper nourishment; nor, again, would John His disciple have said, when writing of Him, "But Jesus, being wearied with the journey, was sitting [to rest];"(10) nor would David have proclaimed of Him beforehand, "They have added to the grief of my wounds;"(11) nor would He have wept over Lazarus, nor have sweated great drops of blood; nor have declared, "My soul is exceeding sorrowful;"(12) nor, when His side was pierced, would there have come forth blood and water. For all these are tokens of the flesh which had been derived from the earth, which He had recapitulated in Himself, bearing salvation to His own handiwork.

3. Wherefore Luke points out that the pedigree which traces the generation of our Lord back to Adam contains seventy–two generations, connecting the end with the beginning, and implying that it is He who has summed up in Himself all nations dispersed from Adam downwards, and all languages and generations of men, together with Adam himself. Hence also was Adam himself termed by Paul "the figure of Him that was to come,"(1) because the Word, the Maker of all things, had formed beforehand for Himself the future dispensation of the human race, connected with the Son of God; God having predestined that the first man should be of an animal nature, with this view, that he might be saved by the spiritual One. For inasmuch as He had a pre–existence as a saving Being, it was necessary that what might be saved should also be called into existence, in order that the Being who saves should not exist in vain.

4. In accordance with this design, Mary the Virgin is found obedient, saying, "Behold the handmaid of the Lord; be it unto me according to thy word."(2) But Eve was disobedient; for she did not obey when as yet she was a virgin. And even as she, having indeed a husband, Adam, but being nevertheless as yet a virgin (for in Paradise "they were both naked, and were not ashamed,"(3) inasmuch as they, having been created a short time previously, had no understanding of the procreation of children: for it was necessary that they should first come to adult age,(4) and then multiply from that time onward), having become disobedient, was made the cause of death, both to herself and to the entire human race; so also did Mary, having a man betrothed [to her], and being nevertheless a virgin, by yielding obedience, become the cause of salvation, both to herself and the whole

human race. And on this account does the law term a woman betrothed to a man, the wife of him who had betrothed her, although she was as yet a virgin; thus indicating the back–reference from Mary to Eve, because what is joined together could not otherwise be put asunder than by inversion of the process by which these bonds of union had arisen; s so that the former ties be cancelled by the latter, that the latter may set the former again at liberty. And it has, in fact, happened that the first compact looses from the

second tie, but that the second tie takes the position of the first which has been cancelled.(6) For this reason did the Lord declare that the first should in truth be last, and the last first.(7) And the prophet, too, indicates the same, saying, "instead of fathers, children have been born unto thee."(8) For the Lord, having been born "the First–begotten of the dead,"(9) and receiving into His bosom the ancient fathers, has regenerated them into the life of God, He having been made Himself the beginning of those that live, as Adam became the beginning of those who die.(10) Wherefore also Luke, commencing the genealogy with the Lord, carried it back to Adam, indicating that it was He who regenerated them into the Gospel of life, and not they Him. And thus also it was that the knot of Eve's disobedience was loosed by the obedience of Mary. For what the virgin Eve had bound fast through unbelief, this did the virgin Mary set free through faith.

CHAP. XXIII.—ARGUMENTS IN OPPOSITION TO TATIAN, SHOWING THAT IT WAS CONSONANT TO DIVINE JUSTICE AND MERCY THAT THE FIRST ADAM SHOULD FIRST PARTAKE IN THAT SALVATION OFFERED TO ALL BY CHRIST.

1. It was necessary, therefore, that the Lord, coming to the lost sheep, and making recapitulation of so comprehensive a dispensation, and seeking after His own handiwork, should save that very man who had been created after His image and likeness, that is, Adam, filling up the times of His condemnation, which had been incurred through disobedience,—[times] "which the Father had placed in His own power."(11) [This was necessary,] too, inasmuch as the whole economy of salvation regarding man came to pass according to the good pleasure of the Father, in order that God might not be conquered, nor His wisdom lessened, [in the estimation of His creatures.] For if man, who had been

created by God that he might live, after losing life, through being injured by the serpent that had corrupted him, should not any more return to life, but should be utterly [and for ever] abandoned to death, God would [in that case] have been conquered, and the wickedness of the serpent would have prevailed over the will of God. But inasmuch as God is invincible and long−suffering, He did indeed show Himself to be long−suffering in the matter of the correction of man and the probation of all, as I have already observed; and by means of the second man did He bind the strong man, and spoiled his goods,(1) and abolished death, vivifying that man who had been in a state of death. For at the first Adam became a vessel in his (Satan's) possession, whom he did also hold under his power, that is, by bringing sin on him iniquitously, and under colour of immortality entailing death upon him. For, while promising that they should be as gods, which was in no way possible for him to be, he wrought death in them: wherefore he who had led man captive, was justly captured in his turn by God; but man, who had been led captive, was loosed from the bonds of condemnation.

2. But this is Adam, if the truth should be told, the first formed man, of whom the Scripture says that the Lord spake, "Let Us make man after Our own image and likeness;"(2) and we are all from him: and as we are from him, therefore have we all inherited his title. But inasmuch as man is saved, it is fitting that he who was created the original man should be saved. For it is too absurd to maintain, that he who was so deeply injured by the enemy, and was the first to suffer captivity, was not rescued by Him who conquered the enemy, but that his children were,—those whom he had begotten in the same captivity. Neither would the enemy appear to be as yet conquered, if the old spoils remained with him. To give an illustration: If a hostile force had overcome certain [enemies], had bound them, and led them away captive, and held them for a long time in servitude, so that they begat children among them; and somebody, compassionating those who had been made slaves, should overcome this same hostile force; he certainly would not act equitably, were he to liberate the children of those who had been led captive, from the sway of those who had enslaved their fathers, but should leave these latter, who had suffered the act of capture, subject to their enemies,—those, too, on whose very account he had proceeded to this retaliation,—the children succeeding to liberty through the avenging of their fathers' cause, but not(3) so that their fathers, who suffered the act of capture itself, should be left [in bondage]. For God is neither devoid of power nor of justice, who has afforded help to man, and restored him to His own liberty.

3. It was for this reason, too, that immediately after Adam had transgressed, as the Scripture relates, He pronounced no curse against Adam

personally, but against the ground, in reference to his works, as a certain person among the ancients has observed: "God did indeed transfer the curse to the earth, that it might not remain in man."(4) But man received, as the punishment of his transgression, the toilsome task of tilling the earth, and to eat bread in the sweat of his face, and to return to the dust from whence he was taken. Similarly also did the woman [receive] toil, and labour, and groans, and the pangs of parturition, and a state of subjection, that is, that she should serve her husband; so that they should neither perish altogether when cursed by God, nor, by remaining unreprimanded, should be led to despise God. But the curse in all its fulness fell upon the serpent, which had beguiled them. "And God," it is declared, "said to the serpent: Because thou hast done this, cubed art thou above all cattle, and above all the beasts of the earth."(5) And this same thing does the Lord also say in the Gospel, to those who are found upon the left hand: "Depart from me, ye cursed, into ever: lasting fire, which my Father hath prepared for the devil and his angels;"(6) indicating that eternal fire was not originally prepared for man, but for him who beguiled man, and caused him to offend—for him, I say, who is chief of the apostasy, and for those angels who became apostates along with him; which [fire], indeed, they too shall justly feel, who, like him, persevere in works of wickedness, without repentance, and without retracing their steps.

4. [These act](7) as Cain [did, who], when he was counselled by God to keep quiet, because he had not made an equitable division of that share to which his brother was entitled, but with envy and malice thought that he could domineer over him, not only did not acquiesce, but even added sin to sin, indicating his state of mind by his action. For what he had planned, that did he also put in practice: he tyrannized over and slew him; God subjecting the just to the unjust, that the former might be proved as the just one by the things which he suffered, and the latter detected as the unjust by those which he perpetrated. And he was not softened even by this, nor did he stop short with that evil deed; but being asked where his brother was, he said, "I know not; am I my brother's keeper?" extending and aggravating [his] wickedness by his answer. For if it is wicked to slay a brother, much worse is it thus insolently and irreverently to reply to the omniscient God as if he could battle Him. And for this he did himself bear a curse about with him, because he gratuitously brought an offering of sin, having had no reverence for God, nor being put to confusion by the act of fratricide.(1)

79

5. The case of Adam, however, had no analogy with this, but was altogether different. For, having been beguiled by another under the pretext of immortality, he is immediately seized with terror, and hides himself; not as if he were able to escape from God; but, in a state of confusion at having transgressed His command, he feels unworthy to appear before and to hold converse with God. Now, "the fear of the Lord is the beginning of wisdom;"(2) the sense of sin leads to repentance, and God bestows His compassion upon those who are penitent. For [Adam] showed his repentance by his conduct, through means of the girdle [which he used], covering himself with fig-leaves, while there were many other leaves, which would have irritated his body in a less degree. He, however, adopted a dress conformable to his disobedience, being awed by the fear of God; and resisting the erring, the lustful propensity of his flesh (since he had lost his natural disposition and child-like mind, and had come to the knowledge of evil things), he girded a bridle of continence upon himself and his wife, fearing God, and waiting for His coming, and indicating, as it were, some such thing [as follows]: Inasmuch as, he says, I have by disobedience lost that robe of sanctity which I had from the Spirit, I do now also acknowledge that I am deserving of a covering of this nature, which affords no gratification, but which gnaws have retained this clothing for ever, thus humbling himself, if God, who is merciful, had not clothed them with tunics of skins instead of fig-leaves. For this purpose, too, He interrogates them, that the blame might light upon the woman; and again, He interrogates her, that she might convey the blame to the serpent. For she related what had occurred. "The serpent," says she, "beguiled me, and I did eat."(3) But He put no question to the serpent; for He knew that he had been the prime mover in the guilty deed; but He pronounced the curse upon him in the first instance, that it might fall upon man with a mitigated rebuke. For God detested him who had led man astray, but by degrees, and little by little, He showed compassion to him who had been beguiled.

6. Wherefore also He drove him out of Paradise, and removed him far from the tree of life, not because He envied him the tree of life, as some venture to assert, but because He pitied

him, [and did not desire] that he should continue a sinner for ever, nor that the sin which surrounded him should be immortal, and evil interminable and irremediable. But He set a bound to his [state of] sin, by interposing death, and thus causing sin to cease,(4) putting an end to it by the dissolution of the flesh, which should take place in the earth, so that man, ceasing at length to live to sin, and dying to it, might begin to live to God.

7. For this end did He put enmity between the serpent and the woman and her seed, they keeping it up mutually: He, the sole of whose foot should be bitten, having power also to tread upon the enemy's head; but the other biting, killing, and impeding the steps of man, until the seed did come appointed to tread down his head,—which was born of Mary, of whom the prophet speaks: "Thou shalt tread upon the asp and the basilisk; thou shalt trample down the lion and the dragon;"(3)—indicating that sin, which was set up and spread out against man, and which rendered him subject to death, should be deprived of its power, along with death, which rules [over men]; and that the lion, that is, antichrist, rampant against mankind in the latter days, should be trampled down by Him; and that He should bind "the dragon, that old serpent"(6) and subject him to the power of man, who had been conquered(7) so that all his might should be trodden down. Now Adam had been conquered, all life having been taken away from him: wherefore, when the foe was conquered in his turn, Adam received new life; and the last enemy, death, is destroyed,(8) which at the first had taken possession of man. Therefore, when man has been liberated, "what is written shall come to pass, Death is swallowed up in victory. O death sting?"(9) This could not be said with justice, if that man, over whom death did first obtain dominion, were not set free. For his salvation is death's destruction. When therefore the Lord vivifies man, that is, Adam, death is at the same time destroyed.

8. All therefore speak falsely who disallow his (Adam's) salvation, shutting themselves out from life for ever, in that they do not believe that the sheep which had perished has been found.(10) For if it has not been found, the whole human race is still held in a state of perdition. False, therefore, is that, man who first started this idea, or rather, this ignorance and blindness—Tatian.(11) As I have already indicated, this man entangled himself with all the heretics.(1) This dogma, however, has been invented by himself, in order that, by introducing something new, independently of the rest, and by speaking vanity. he might acquire for himself hearers void of faith, affecting to be esteemed a teacher, and endeavouring from time to time to employ sayings of this kind often [made use of] by Paul: "In Adam we all die;"(2) ignorant, however, that "where sin abounded, grace did much more abound."(3) Since this, then, has been clearly shown, let all his disciples be put to shame, and let them wrangle(4) about Adam, as if some great gain were to accrue to them if he be not saved; when they profit nothing more [by that], even as the serpent also did not profit when persuading man [to sin], except to this effect, that he proved him a transgressor, obtaining man as the first–fruits of his own apostasy.(5) But he did not know God's power.(6) Thus also do those who disallow Adam's salvation gain nothing, except this, that they render themselves heretics and apostates from the

truth, and show themselves patrons of the serpent and of death.

CHAP. XXIV.—RECAPITULATION OF THE VARIOUS ARGUMENTS ADDUCED AGAINST GNOSTIC IMPIETY UNDER ALL ITS ASPECTS. THE HERETICS, TOSSED ABOUT BY EVERY BLAST OF DOCTRINE, ARE OPPOSED BY THE UNIFORM TEACHING OF THE CHURCH, WHICH REMAINS SO ALWAYS, AND IS CONSISTENT WITH ITSELF.

1. Thus, then, have all these men been exposed, who bring in impious doctrines regarding our Maker and Framer, who also formed this world. and above whom there is no other God and those have been overthrown by their own arguments who teach falsehoods regarding the substance of our Lord, and the dispensation which He fulfilled for the sake of His own creature man. But [it has, on the other hand, been shown], that the preaching of the Church is everywhere consistent, and continues in an even course, and receives testimony from the prophets, the apostles, and all the disciples—as I have proved—through [those in] the beginning, the middle, and the end,(7) and through the entire dispensation of God, and that well–grounded system which tends(8) to man's salvation, namely, our faith; which, having been received from the Church, we do preserve, and which always, by the Spirit of God, renewing its youth, as if it were some precious deposit in an excellent vessel, causes the vessel itself containing it to renew its youth also. For this gift of God has been entrusted to the Church, as breath was to the first created man,(9) for this purpose, that all the members receiving it may be vivified; and the [means of] communion with Christ has been distributed throughout it, that is, the Holy Spirit, the earnest of incorruption, the means of confirming our faith, and the ladder of ascent to God. "For in the Church," it is said, "God hath set apostles, prophets, teachers,"(10) and all

the other means through which the Spirit works; of which all those are not partakers who do not join themselves to the Church, but defraud themselves of life through their perverse opinions and infamous behaviour. For where the Church is, there is the Spirit of God; and where the Spirit of God is, there is the Church, and every kind of grace; but the Spirit is truth. Those, therefore, who do not partake of Him, are neither nourished into life from the mother's breasts, nor do they enjoy that most limpid fountain which issues from the body of Christ; but they dig for themselves broken cisterns(11) out of earthly trenches, and drink putrid water out of the mire, fleeing from the faith of the Church lest they be convicted; and rejecting the Spirit, that they may not be instructed.

2. Alienated thus from the truth, they do deservedly wallow in all error, tossed to and fro by it, thinking differently in regard to the same things at different times, and never attaining to a well–grounded knowledge, being more anxious to be sophists of words than disciples of the truth. For they have not been founded upon the one rock, but upon the sand, which has in itself a multitude of stones. Wherefore they also imagine many gods, and they always have the excuse of searching [after truth] (for they are blind), but never succeed in finding it. For they blaspheme the Creator, Him who is truly God, who also furnishes power to find [the truth]; imagining that they have discovered another god beyond God, or another Pleroma, or another dispensation. Wherefore also the light which is from God does not illumine them, because they have dishonoured and despised God, holding Him of small account, because, through His love and infinite benignity, He has come within reach of human knowledge (knowledge, however, not with regard to His greatness, · or with regard to His essence—for that has no man measured or handled—but after this sort: that we should know that He who made, and formed, and breathed in them the breath of life, and nourishes us by means of the creation, establishing all things by His Word, and binding them together by His Wisdom(1)—this is He who is the only true God); but they dream of a non–existent being above Him, that they may be regarded as having found out the great God, whom nobody, [they hold,] can recognise holding communication with the human race, or as directing mundane matters: that is to say, they find out the god of Epicurus, who does nothing either for himself or others; that is, he exercises no providence at all.

CHAP. XXV.—THIS WORLD IS RULED PROVIDENCE OF ONE GOD, WHO IS BOTH ENDOWED WITH INFINITE JUSTICE TO PUNISH THE WICKED, AND WITH INFINITE GOODNESS TO BLESS THE PIOUS, AND IMPART TO THEM SALVATION.

1. God does, however, exercise a providence over all things, and therefore He also gives

counsel; and when giving counsel, He is present with those who attend to moral discipline.(2) It follows then of course, that the things which are watched over and governed should be acquainted with their ruler; which things are not irrational or vain, but they have understanding derived from the providence of God. And, for this reason certain of the Gentiles, who were less addicted to [sensual] allurements and voluptuousness, and were not led away to such a degree of superstition with regard to idols, being moved, though but slightly, by His providence, were nevertheless convinced that they should call the Maker of this universe the Father, who exercises a providence over all things, and arranges the affairs of our world.

2. Again, that they might remove the rebuking and judicial power from the Father, reckoning that as unworthy of God, and thinking that they had found out a God both without anger and [merely] good, they have alleged that one [God] judges, but that another saves, unconsciously taking away the intelligence and justice of both deities. For if the judicial one is not also good, to bestow favours upon the deserving, and to direct reproofs against those requiring them, he will appear neither a just nor a wise judge. On the other hand, the good God, if he is merely good, and not one who tests those upon whom he shall send his goodness, will be out of the range of justice and goodness; and his goodness will seem imperfect, as not saving all; [for it should do so,] if it be not accompanied with judgment.

3. Marcion, therefore, himself, by dividing God into two, maintaining one to be good and the other judicial, does in fact, on both sides, put an end to deity. For he that is the judicial one, if he be not good, is not God, because he from whom goodness is absent is no God at all; and again, he who is good, if he has no judicial power, suffers the same [loss] as the former, by being deprived of his character of deity. And how can they call the Father of all wise, if they do not assign to Him a judicial faculty? For if He is wise, He is also one who tests [others]; but the judicial power belongs to him who tests, and justice follows the judicial faculty, that it may reach a just conclusion; justice calls forth judgment, and judgment, when it is executed with justice, will pass on to wisdom. Therefore the Father will excel in wisdom all human and angelic wisdom, because He is Lord, and Judge, and the Just One, and Ruler over all. For He is good, and merciful, and patient, and saves whom He ought: nor does goodness desert Him in the exercise of justice,(3) nor is His wisdom lessened; for He saves those whom He should save, and judges those worthy of judgment. Neither does He show Himself unmercifully just; for His goodness, no doubt, goes on before, and takes precedency.

4. The God, therefore, who does benevolently cause His sun to rise upon all,(4) and sends rain upon the just and unjust, shall judge those who, enjoying His equally distributed kindness, have led lives not corresponding to the dignity of His bounty; but who have spent their days in wantonness and luxury, in opposition to His benevolence, and have, moreover, even blasphemed Him who has conferred so great benefits upon them.

5. Plato is proved to be more religious than these men, for he allowed that the same God was both just and good, having power over all things, and Himself executing judgment, expressing himself thus, "And God indeed, as He is also the ancient Word, possessing the beginning, the end, and the mean of all existing things, does everything rightly, moving round about them according to their nature; but retributive justice always follows Him against those who depart from the divine law."(5) Then, again, he points out that the Maker and Framer of the universe is good. "And to the good," he says, "no envy ever springs up with regard to anything;"(6) thus establishing the goodness of God, as the beginning and the cause of the creation of the world, but not ignorance, nor an erring Aeon, nor the consequence of a defect, nor the Mother weeping and lamenting, nor another God or Father.

6. Well may their Mother bewail them, as capable of conceiving and inventing such things for they have worthily uttered this falsehood against themselves, that their Mother is beyond the Pleroma, that is beyond the knowledge of God, and that their entire multitude became(1) a shapeless and crude abortion: for it apprehends nothing of the truth; it falls into void and darkness: for their wisdom (Sophia) was void, and wrapped up in darkness; and Horos did not permit her to enter the Pleroma: for the Spirit (Achamoth) did not receive them into the place of refreshment. For their father, by begetting ignorance, wrought in them the sufferings of death. We do not misrepresent [their opinions on] these points; but they do themselves confirm, they do themselves teach, they do glory in them, they imagine a lofty [mystery] about their Mother, whom they represent as having been begotten without a father, that is, without God, a female from a female,(2) that is, corruption from error.

7. We do indeed pray that these men may not remain in the pit which they themselves have dug, but separate themselves from a Mother of this nature, and depart from Bythus, and stand away from the void, and relinquish the shadow; and that they, being converted to the Church of God, may be lawfully begotten, and that Christ may be formed in them, and that they may know the Framer and Maker of this universe, the only true God and

Lord of all. We pray for these things on their behalf, loving them better than they seem to love themselves. For our love, inasmuch as it is true, is salutary to them, if they will but receive it. It may be compared to a severe remedy, extirpating the proud and sloughing flesh of a wound; for it puts an end to their pride and haughtiness. Wherefore it shall not weary us, to endeavour with all our might to stretch out the hand unto them. Over and above what has been already stated, I have deferred to the following book, to adduce the words of the Lord; if, by convincing some among them, through means of the very instruction of Christ, I may succeed in persuading them to abandon such error, and to cease from blaspheming their Creator, who is both God alone, and the Father of our Lord Jesus Christ. Amen.

ELUCIDATION

THE editor of this American Series confines himself in general to such occasional and very brief annotations as may suggest to students and others the practical views which are requisite to a clear comprehension of authors who wrote for past ages; for a sort and condition of men no longer existing, whose extinction as a class is, indeed, largely due to these writings. But he reserved to himself the privilege of correcting palpable mistakes, especially in points which bear upon questions of our own times.

That our learned translators have unaccountably admitted a very inaccurate translation of the crucial paragraph in book iii. cap. iii. sect. 2, I have shown in the footnote at that place. It is evident,(1) because they themselves are not satisfied with it, and(2) because I have set it side by side with the more literal rendering of a writer who would have preferred their reading if it could have borne the test of criticism.

Now, the authors of the Latin translation(1) may have designed the ambiguity which gives the Ultramontane party an apparent advantage; but it is an advantage which disappears as soon as it is examined, and hence I am content to take it as it stands. Various conjectures have been made as to the original Greek of Irenaeus; but the Latin answers every purpose of the author's argument, and is fatal to the claims of the Papacy. Let me recur to the translation given, in loco, from a Roman Catholic, and this will be seen at once. For he thus renders it:—

1. In this Church, "ever, by those who are on every side, has been preserved that tradition which is from apostles." How would such a proposition have sounded to Pius IX. in the

Vatican Council? The faith is preserved by those who come to Rome, not by the Bishop who presides there.

2. "For to this Church, on account of more potent principality,(1) it is necessary that every Church (that is, those who are, on every side, faithful) resort." The greatness of Rome, that is, as the capital of the Empire, imparts to the local Church a superior dignity, even as compared with Lyons, or any other metropolitical Church. Everybody visits Rome: hence you find there faithful witnesses from every side (from all the Churches); and their united testimony it is which preserves in Rome the pure apostolic traditions.

The Latin, thus translated by a candid Roman Catholic, reverses the whole system of the Papacy. Pius IX. informed his Bishops, at the late Council, that they were not called to bear their testimony, but to hear his infallible decree; "reducing us," said the Archbishop of Paris, "to a council of sacristans."

Sustaining these views by a few footnotes, I add(1) a literal rendering of my own, and then(2) a metaphrase of the same, bringing out the argument from the crabbed obstructions of the Latin text. This, then, is what Irenaeus says: (a) "For it is necessary for every Church (that is to say, the faithful from all parts) to meet in this Church, on account of the superior magistracy; in which Church, by those who are from all places, the tradition of the apostles has been preserved." Or, more freely rendered: (b) "On account of the chief magistracy(2) [of the empire], the faithful from all parts, representing every Church, are obliged to resort to Rome, and there to come together; so that [it is the distinction of this Church that], in it, the tradition of the apostles has been preserved by Christians gathered together out of all the Churches." Taking the entire argument of our author with the context, then, it amounts to this: "We must ask, not for local, but universal, testimony. Now, in every Church founded by the apostles has been handed down their traditions; but, as it would be a tedious thing to collect them all, let this suffice. Take that Church (nearest at hand, and which is the only Apostolic Church of the West), the great and glorious Church at Rome, which was there founder by the two apostles Peter and Paul. In her have been preserved the traditions of all the Churches, because everybody is forced to go to the seat of empire: and therefore, by these representatives of the whole Catholic Church, the apostolic traditions have been all collected in Rome:(3) and you have a synoptical view of all Churches in what is there preserved." Had the views of the modern Papacy ever entered the head of Irenaeus, what an absurdity would be this whole argument. He would have said, "It is no matter what may be gathered elsewhere; for the Bishop of Rome is the infallible oracle of all Catholic truth, and you will always find it by his mouth." It should be noted that Orthodoxy was indeed preserved there, just so long as Rome permitted other Churches to contribute their testimony on the principle of Irenaeus, and thus to make her the depository of all Catholic tradition, as witnessed "by all, everywhere, and from the beginning." But all this is turned upside down by modern Romanism. No other Church is to be heard or considered; but Rome takes all into her own power, and may dictate to all Churches what they are to believe, however novel, or contrary to the torrent of antiquity in the teachings of their own founders and great doctors in all past time.

Printed in the United States
59526LVS00005B/42